GREAT DAY IN THE MORNING

Thomas Babe

BROADWAY PLAY PUBLISHING INC
New York
www.broadwayplaypublishing.com
info@broadwayplaypublishing.com

GREAT DAY IN THE MORNING
© Copyright 1998 Thomas Babe

All rights reserved. This work is fully protected under the copyright laws of the United States of America. No part of this publication may be photocopied, reproduced, stored in a retrieval system, or transmitted, in any form or by any means, electronic, mechanical, recording, or otherwise, without the prior permission of the publisher. Additional copies of this play are available from the publisher.

Written permission is required for live performance of any sort. This includes readings, cuttings, scenes, and excerpts. For amateur and stock performances, please contact Broadway Play Publishing Inc. For all other rights please contact the author's estate c/o B P P I.

Cover photo compliments South Coast Repertory
I S B N: 978-0-88145-144-3
First edition: September 1998
Book design: Marie Donovan
Copy editing 1997: Liam Brosnahan
Page make-up: Adobe InDesign
Typeface: Palatino

GREAT DAY IN THE MORNING opened 26 February 1993 at South Coast Repertory. The cast and creative contributors were:

ELIZABETH	Gloria Biegler
ULYSSES S GRANT	Douglas Rowe
HARRY LEHR	Michael Brian
JOHNNIE GOODENOUGH	Jerome Butler
MRS LUCY WHARTON DREXEL	Jane A Johnson
MRS STUYVESANT FISH	Pamela Dunlop
MRS CAROLINE ASTOR	Oceana Marr
CHARLIE	Alan Brooks
Pianist	John Ellington
Director	David Emmes
Scenic design	Gerard Howland
Costumes	Walker Hicklin
Lighting	Peter Maradudin
Original music, music direction, & sound design	Michael Roth
Choreography	Sylvia C Turner
Literary advisor	Jerry Patch
Production stage manager	Bonnie Lorenger

The production received a grant from the Fund for New American Plays, Kennedy Center, Washington, DC.

CHARACTERS

ELIZABETH, *early thirties, a widow*
ULYSSES S GRANT, *sixties, public figure*
HARRY LEHR, *thirties, society man*
JOHNNIE GOODENOUGH, *late twenties,* HARRY's *black manservant*
MRS LUCY WHARTON DREXEL, *sixties,* ELIZABETH's *mother*
MRS STUYVESANT FISH, *forties, society woman*
MRS CAROLINE ASTOR, *sixties, society's leader*
CHARLIE, *thirties, society dropout*

Fashionable locales along the eastern seaboard; some time near the turn of the century

To the memory of my father, and his good Irish ways

It's morning in America.

President Ronald Reagan

ACT ONE

Scene One

(Jewel box 19th century stage with red curtains and gold trim. Fanfare from a small orchestra off stage introduces JOHNNIE GOODENOUGH *in fancy evening clothes, with cane and top hat.)*

JOHNNIE: Ladies and gentlemen all. No summer nights in no fine houses in Atlanta could ever be said to be complete without the belle you have been waiting for to hear. The champagne now has been put away for the evening—enjoy your last small sip—and someone back in the big rooms is tiptoeing about, pinching out the candles. So when the song has done, you had best steal off to your coach-and-fours and leave us to clear up the tables so we all get to sleep before the sun peers over the edge of the world again and it's already the next day's work. If that's just fine, then, I'm proud to offer, on her last viewing before her grand departure to New York, land of big dollars and bad Yankees, our own, our best—the greatest lady performer of Georgia—herself in person!

(Opening strains of A Bird in A Gilded Cage *as the lady, in a very fine dress, enters sexily and sings)*

LADY: The ballroom was filled with fashion's throng,
It shone with a thousand lights,
And there was a woman who passed along,
The fairest of all the sights.

A girl to her lover then softly sighed,
There's riches at her command;
But she married for wealth, not for love, he cried,
Though she lives in a mansion grand.

She's only a bird in a gilded cage,
A beautiful sight to see,
You may think she's happy and free from care,
She's not, though she seems to be.

'Tis sad when you think of her wasted life,
For youth cannot mate with age,
And her beauty was sold for an old man's gold,
She's a bird in a gilded cage.

(On the final note, the lady takes her wig off, revealing HARRY LEHR, *who bows deeply and sweetly. Blackout)*

Scene Two

(A yacht steaming up the Hudson. At the rail is GENERAL GRANT, *smoking a cigar. With him,* ELIZABETH. *Music from the salon drifts in, from time to time.)*

ELIZABETH: *(Singing)*
She's only a bird in a gilded cage,
A beautiful sight to see….

GRANT: That's a whore song.

ELIZABETH: It has a catchy melody.

GRANT: So does "Dixie."

ELIZABETH: *(A little raucous)* Oh, I wish I was in de land ob cotton—

GRANT: Bessie, for heaven's sake, this is a rather nice little jaunt we're having around Manhattan's island, on a rather nice boat some folks invited us to partake of. Rather nice people are on board, too, the sort you've

ACT ONE 3

been hoping to meet. In fact, you are one of the rather nice people yourself.

ELIZABETH: Yes, I am, am't I?

GRANT: And you recently lost a husband.

ELIZABETH: Not *so* recently.

GRANT: People expect you to be demure, downcast, a little, please?

ELIZABETH: Yes. And people expect me still to cry.

GRANT: They have every right.

ELIZABETH: Well, dear General, I feel it all keenly on this vast and mighty Hudson, rolling down upon us from God-knows-what tiny streams and little hamlets and unknown homesteads, and by it goes and on it goes and sometimes I do want to weep, yes, that's true.

GRANT: Good.

ELIZABETH: I forestall my tears, however, by thinking of God and looking at the handsome young men who parade down Broadway.

GRANT: You do both things simultaneously?

ELIZABETH: They are approximately, in my estimation, the same subject.

GRANT: Then, just be careful you don't become a lunatic.

ELIZABETH: I am just looking at them, General, I am not acting upon them. Meantime, you wanted to show me something…?

GRANT: *(Pointing out)* It's coming up right over there, you see, above the bank where those naked little boys are jumping off the log and into that muddy estuary.

ELIZABETH: All made of marble, I suppose?

GRANT: Of course, all made of marble. Did you think they'd make it of wood?

ELIZABETH: And you're to be planted there in a box fashioned out of iron and lined with zinc so the worm will corrupt not?

GRANT: I hadn't thought about that part.

ELIZABETH: You'd better.

GRANT: Why are you going on and on about all the sordid details?

ELIZABETH: You're the one had to show me where your tomb is going to be.

GRANT: Well, I wanted to share my future with you. Everybody's got to sleep somewhere when they're gone. And, in this matter, I get more choice than I've had in most of the rest.

(As ELIZABETH speaks, HARRY drifts on, leaning over the rail a little way away and staring out.)

ELIZABETH: My late husband, whom you admired so much, as did the rest of the world, is sleeping—if that's the right word and in his case, I'm sure it is—in Colorado. We went there for his health, but when we arrived, I discovered most people had come to die. They didn't say that just. But the women I met were all buying black dresses and planning their widowhoods while their husbands sat on a variety of verandas and coughed and spat and turned paler and paler. John was good, he was very good, he was fine for a while, with his iron-clad faith in God's infinite mercy, and then there was a long, cold, wet, dark spell and one night I cradled his beautiful head and he just went away. And with him, I think, went my youth.

GRANT: That's a load of crap, Bessie. You're still very young and you will live a very long time. Women do. Make something of it.

ACT ONE

ELIZABETH: Why do you think I took up a house of my own in New York? I need to begin again. So I don't want you to turn all proper on me and tell me to mind my manners.

GRANT: You're the damn proper one here and you always have been, owing in large part, I believe, to your mother's strict instruction. After all, I'm just a friend of the family. So you can always tell me to mind my own business.

ELIZABETH: I wonder. Are you really the tough old bird you'd like me to think of you as, or does a kinder, more feminine heart, which you hide, beat inwardly?

GRANT: *(Embarrassed)* Get on with you, Bessie. That son-of-a-bitch Douglas once accused old Abe Lincoln of being two-faced, and Lincoln said to him, You think if I had another, I'd wear this one?

HARRY: *(Moving over, interrupting)* Excuse me, General Grant?

GRANT: Do I owe you money?

HARRY: No.

GRANT: Does my no-good, hapless, but much-adored son owe you money?

HARRY: No.

GRANT: Then good day, laddy-bucks.

HARRY: I'm sorry to have broken into your colloquy, sir. It wasn't you I had in mind. I simply wanted to pay my compliments to your daughter.

GRANT: My…

ELIZABETH: Daughter!

(They both laugh.)

HARRY: *(Making to leave)* Well, I guess I was foolish. I apologize for any inconvenience I may have caused.

GRANT: No, wait. Let's hear the compliment. My daughter here likes a good compliment.

ELIZABETH: *(Playing along)* Pa-pa!

GRANT: Come on, son. Don't be shy.

HARRY: Well, then, let me begin by saying, so that the General won't shoot me, that though I am from the South, I am too young by far to have participated in the recent disagreement between the states…

GRANT: Forgiven. We didn't feel it necessary to kill off all the babies of those we conquered. And…?

HARRY: We are famous, at the South, for the beauty of our women…

GRANT: Yes. Yes. Common knowledge you think so. More matter.

HARRY: On the summer evenings, you hear their dresses rustle, you look up and see a glint of gold as the moonlight catches their fair tresses, you smell the perfume of their bodies intermingled with the jasmine and the heliotrope and then you happen to look into their eyes and…it is like looking into nothing.

GRANT: You were unlucky in love, I take it?

ELIZABETH: Shh, Pa-pa. I'm listening!

HARRY: Well, you have a point, it may be true of most women everywhere. But then, on a sudden instance, you encounter one of the rare birds, as it were, whose eyes are a window into a soul of such purity and unutterable beauty that it takes one's breath away. That is what has happened to me here, today, on this innocent afternoon. *(Pause)* That's all I have to say.

GRANT: Well, isn't that a hell of a note!

ELIZABETH: Papa! What this gentleman has said is very sweet, even if it is inflation.

ACT ONE 7

HARRY: Hardly that. With your permission, may I call on you?

ELIZABETH: Though, as a matter of fact, I am not General Grant's daughter?

HARRY: *(Presenting his card)* Especially if you are not General Grant's daughter.

ELIZABETH: I am Mrs John Dahlgren, a widow… *(Reading the card)* Mister Harry Lehr. You may call on me, if you wish, and if you can take the trouble to find where I live.

HARRY: I believe I can.

ELIZABETH: Then I feel obliged to warn you, I am a very strict person.

HARRY: Fine. So am I. Good day, then. I have to rejoin my party. It is made up of people less interesting than yourselves. But, then, you see, I am beholden to them, as I am not to you. *(Exits)*

ELIZABETH: I don't think he's a very strict person.

GRANT: Well, I don't imagine I'd ever approve of any man who made advances toward you.

ELIZABETH: So few ever have. But I rather liked this one.

GRANT: I just don't know….

ELIZABETH: You don't have to. I'm the one. And now I've made the giant step—I mean, for me, it is giant—from that little old safe city I was raised in off in the wilds of Pennsylvania to this big and thrilling Gomorrah, don't you think I'd better begin to make some use of it?

GRANT: For what?

ELIZABETH: Something bigger than I have ever known. Something which will be my own and not just handed to me. Something filled with great passion.

GRANT: Oh, Bessie, please. You read that in one of those romantical ladies' novels.

ELIZABETH: So what if I did? Do you know of another way I should approach the situation?

GRANT: Like a war. The kind we fought. We took what we could when we could, where and how we could find it, and waited until much later to decide what it had all meant.

ELIZABETH: I could never live like that.

GRANT: Everything I ever cared for in my life I couldn't have, but I made something out of it anyway. *(Watching the river)* Look at the water, my dear. It doesn't pay much attention to anything, least of all us. It scares the living bejesus out of me.

ELIZABETH: My word! And here I was thinking I'd love to jump right into it.

(A ship's bell rings.)

GRANT: I believe we're docking. Would you like to get on with it now?

ELIZABETH: I would be so pleased.

(Blackout)

Scene Three

(The drawing room of ELIZABETH's home. She sits, writing in her diary.)

ELIZABETH: "Mr Lehr, who has seen me twice now and each time better than the last, has qualities I have grown to like. I do believe he is different than most of the rest…." *(Crosses out)* "…different *from* most of the rest…" *(Crosses out)* "…different from *all* of the rest, save the General. What a strange time we live in, that men should get smaller in size as they get larger in their powers—"

(MRS DREXEL, ELIZABETH's *mother, enters.* ELIZABETH *hides her diary.)*

ELIZABETH: Mama…are you feeling better?

MRS DREXEL: No.

ELIZABETH: I'm sorry.

MRS DREXEL: It's quite likely I will never feel altogether better again. I don't like the city. I have no friends here, or, I should say, despite my wealth and social lines, I am not quite good enough to have friends, except old invalids like myself who are all considered very out of step with the young nobs and swells who now lord it up so regally.

ELIZABETH: You shouldn't let them drive you away.

MRS DREXEL: But they all waste so much on their cotillions and balls and picnics and summer homes and coaching parties and weddings and luncheons and those terrible paintings of dragons being knocked for a loop by skinny little French chevaliers….

ELIZABETH: Mama, please. It takes all your strength to hate them. The money they spend benefits everyone as it runs down in tiny rivulets to the greengrocers and couturiers and even the ragged little boys who sell the newspapers that tell about them. Besides, the fruits of their ambition and labor provide an example to thousands of less fortunate people who might not, otherwise, strive so hard to better themselves.

MRS DREXEL: You think all that could possibly be true?

ELIZABETH: I have been told.

MRS DREXEL: Hmm. Well, I have been told something, too, Bessie. The men don't like this fellow very much, the one who is so typical of the whole ruck.

ELIZABETH: This fellow? And who, on earth, is this fellow?

MRS DREXEL: You know well enough. They say he has no money. They call him one of the little brothers of the rich. *(Pause)* I think you should come back to Pennsylvania with me.

ELIZABETH: You know that's impossible.

MRS DREXEL: Why is it impossible? Nothing's impossible. We are both widows. We have both outlived men whose peer we shall not see again. We both know other men could never be half as good and most of them are no good whatsoever. You'll find a gentleman near Pen Ryn who may have a lower temperature than some of the overheated stallions here, but he will be honest, at least, and carry you along. What is impossible about that?

ELIZABETH: Here is all the world I care about now.

MRS DREXEL: And you are always pretending to my face that you are tough enough to survive. I don't think you are. Anyone tough enough to survive all this has given up any claim to being a lady.

ELIZABETH: You never hear a good thing I have had to say about my life in New York. None of that stays with you.

MRS DREXEL: It stays, my dear, it stays and goes way within, where it wreaks terrible havoc on my failing organs.

ELIZABETH: You can't do this to me.

MRS DREXEL: I'm afraid I can. It is part of my contract, the one I made with our Redeemer, that I would see at

ACT ONE 11

least one child of mine properly lodged in the bowels of a Christian contentment.

ELIZABETH: You do understand, I hope, that I will never—and I underline the word never—

MRS DREXEL: Do you underline the word "never" in your secret little diary?

ELIZABETH: *(Ignoring this)* I will never disgrace you or make you unhappy, ever, because I love you. It is the way I was raised and the way I will die, but….

MRS DREXEL: Now comes the "but." Do you underline that word, too?

ELIZABETH: Inside of me is something I know nothing about except that it makes me very restless sometimes. And it must be listened to or I will end up…

MRS DREXEL: Like me?

ELIZABETH: I didn't mean that.

MRS DREXEL: Of course, you did. We all have something inside, Bessie, and most times it had better stay there, to be kept and watched and not fed, or, when we least expect it, it will rear up and bite us on the backside.

ELIZABETH: *(Regaining her composure)* When will you be leaving then?

MRS DREXEL: Tomorrow. I am returning home to die. I hope you can come visit before.

ELIZABETH: I shall. Otherwise, when you finally do go to your reward, I'm certain you'll come back and haunt me.

MRS DREXEL: Well, you must be happy. I know that. I want that for you, too, to see you again radiant. But to be happy, remember, hew to the proven truths. Never give yourself up secretly. Never lie. Never divorce from any man to whom you have pledged your everlasting troth. Then, in heaven, is our only glory.

ELIZABETH: And our golden harp.

HARRY: *(O S. Singing jauntily)*
You can dig my grave with a silver spade,
You can dig my grave with a silver spade....

(ELIZABETH *and* MRS DREXEL *look at each other.)*

HARRY: *(O S)*
You can dig my grave with a silver spade...
(Enters) 'Cause I ain't gonna be here much longer!
(Pause) My good women, thus I find you!

ELIZABETH: Mister Lehr.

MRS DREXEL: Good afternoon, young man. Don't you have a job?

HARRY: Yes, I do, Mrs Drexel, I have a job. My job is to find women like yourself—of wise maturity and astonishing experience—and when I see they are down in the dumps, then my job is to create something to cheer them up.

MRS DREXEL: You can't cheer me up with flippancy.

HARRY: Can I cheer you up if I tell you that you have nurtured a daughter of exquisite beauty, refinement and—what is most important to me—a high morality?

MRS DREXEL: You might bring a smile to my face going in that direction, yes, if I believed what you said.

HARRY: Very well, I will offer you my bona fides. I am going to tell you something—because your attention matters to me—that I have never told anyone before, not even Miss Elizabeth here, whom I respect with a confidence. When I was a much younger man, my family was very rich. Then, one morning, my father was dead. Quite unexpectedly dead. We were shaken to our very souls. We scratched under rocks and searched through drawers and cut open all the mattresses and there was no money anywhere. None. So, our horses were taken, our pictures, our furniture and, finally, our dwelling place itself. We lived in shame. My mother sewed, when she was not weeping. My sister cooked in a low-rent boarding house. I was clerk in a bank, keeping track of other men's wealth. And all that while, what saved us, what saved me especially, was my belief—which my father had instilled in me—that in this great age of triumph, of treasure dug up from the earth and titanic manufactures and, eventually, an American empire that could, and will, reach around the Earth—I would succeed because I could find opportunities. But, because of who I am and how I was raised, I should never exploit another human being. I must be honest and square, as I have been taught, always and with every man, and as I am being, now, with you.

MRS DREXEL: *(Dazed)* You remind me of my late husband, Bessie's father. Are all interesting men like you?

HARRY: Dear God, I hope not.

MRS DREXEL: This day and age, I think they are. Well…

HARRY: With your permission, I am going to get Little Miss Bessie out of the house again today and see if we can find something to do even more amusing than yesterday.

MRS DREXEL: You don't need my permission, I've been told over and over again.

HARRY: It would matter.

MRS DREXEL: You have it. Bessie?

ELIZABETH: My word, for a moment, I thought I wasn't here. Do you suppose I could find something a bit more suitable to wear?

HARRY: Please.

ELIZABETH: Thank you. *(Exits)*

MRS DREXEL: *(Eyeing* HARRY*)* If I were a little younger...

HARRY: Yes?

MRS DREXEL: I wouldn't marry you, Mister Lehr. I wouldn't even accept your favors. But I'd keep you somewhere nearby, maybe in a little cage in the drawing room. And you would always be well taken care of.

HARRY: In other words, you don't know what to make of me? Well, if it's any comfort, I don't know what to make of myself, either.

MRS DREXEL: *(Suddenly dead on)* Is that so? Truly so? Be very careful, Mister Lehr. God is watching you.

(MRS DREXEL *turns and goes. Fade slowly on* HARRY, *lighting a cigar, singing)*

HARRY:
There's a long white robe up in heaven for me,
There's a long white robe up in heaven for me,
There's a long white robe up in heaven for me,
'Cause I ain't gonna be here much longer.

(Blackout)

Scene Four

(Fifth Avenue at night. The big window of a mansion behind shows silhouettes of men and women at a party. Music and laughter from inside fills the street as ELIZABETH *and* HARRY *enter.)*

ELIZABETH: It was such fun to go to Barnum's museum, though I do wonder, Harry, if the woman they had on

ACT ONE 15

display there could possibly have had real hair on her face.

HARRY: *(Loving this)* On her chest, too, I believe.

ELIZABETH: Oh, no! And what was the other place, where that emaciated black man played the piano like a drunken angel?

HARRY: A private club where some of the better boys hang out.

ELIZABETH: Well, I have never seen, though I have heard about, of course, such wonders. *(Noticing the party inside)* Harry, look! Inside there! The people are dancing the night away. Does no one ever sleep in this city?

HARRY: I was invited to that one, don't'cha know.

ELIZABETH: Oh, good. Let's stop in a moment.

HARRY: It's late. Your poor mother will be burning a candle in the window, awaiting your return.

ELIZABETH: *(Tugging on his arm)* But they're having such a swell bash, they don't care what time it is. Why should we?

HARRY: They're quite far down the ladder, these people. They barely qualify. And I'm not ready to announce you yet.

ELIZABETH: *(Good humored)* I beg your pardon? I don't need to be announced. Anywhere, Mister Lehr. I am simply your friend, that's all.

HARRY: You are more than that.

ELIZABETH: Am I? How did I get to be more than your friend? I am not society.

HARRY: But I think you could be.

ELIZABETH: *(Sudden enthusiasm)* Not if I don't know what it's all about. Couldn't we just pop in briefly?

HARRY: As I said, it won't do. They're not really the inner circle, the Four Hundred or so names who are socially acceptable, a list I helped create and refine with Mrs Astor—

ELIZABETH: Oh, my, *the* Mrs Astor.

HARRY: Her, exactly. And in that circle of hers there are only about one hundred and fifty names which are truly golden. There are another nineteen or so, by my last count, who matter in a pinch, another twenty-six we can put up with, then another, perhaps, forty-nine, who might qualify if you are throwing a somewhat larger soiree and have room for them, and another one hundred and fifty-six exactly who are needed to make a truly grand event stupendous. They are all millionaires and they all have pretensions and many of them will never know, if they even bother to guess, where they really stand.

ELIZABETH: You sound like God, Harry, calling the roll of the saved and the nearly saved and, finally, the eternally doomed. Where does my family fit into all of this?

HARRY: Nowhere.

ELIZABETH: Good. I must tell you now, I have no social ambitions whatsoever.

HARRY: But I really would, with your permission, like to change all of that.

ELIZABETH: What if I like the way I am now?

HARRY: You tell me: Were your mother and father ever happy? I can ask this because I realize now that mine never were.

ELIZABETH: My father is dead.

HARRY: I know that. I know your father is dead. I know your husband is dead. I know that your mother—God

ACT ONE

bless her—is barely alive. They all lived decent lives with their lips pressed tightly together. But were they really ever, just once, in a way they could describe without blushing…happy?

ELIZABETH: I don't know. I don't even know if they ever planned on having their lives summed up so easily in a word.

HARRY: Would you mind, then, if I asked you the same question?

ELIZABETH: Not in the world. I have been happy, yes. Gallantly happy. Quietly, calmly happy. But I have never known…rapture.

HARRY: It is not too late.

ELIZABETH: Are you saying that, in order to know true happiness, I shall have to join this wonderful inner circle?

HARRY: Look about you, my dear. Up and down this glorious Fifth Avenue—the little houses being thrown down to make way for the bigger houses, the bigger houses being added onto—palaces, chateaus, castles all cast in gilt and marble. I want to have one of those myself someday and sit inside with my devoted wife and my beautiful children, or my beautiful wife and my devoted children, and be alone in the evening to look out the window and think deeply about the folly of having wanted to own such a big mansion in the first place.

ELIZABETH: So do I, Harry, I want exactly that, too. Isn't it wonderful that we are friends?

HARRY: It's the best thing. Shall we dance?

ELIZABETH: Oh, please. But don't hold me too close. I'm not ready for that, yet.

HARRY: Because it would be rapture?

(ELIZABETH *and* HARRY *assume waltz positions and take some grand steps together. As the music from inside becomes faster, they pull closer together.* GRANT *shuffles on, drunk and singing.)*

GRANT: Daisy, Daisy, give me your answer, do! I'm half crazy—

ELIZABETH: General! You're half-drunk, is what you are!

GRANT: Am I, then? I probably am. I was at my club, trying to write in private a little memoir about the war, when some of the fellahs popped by and plied me with strong waters. They wanted to honor me, they said. I said, For what? They said, For killing some many of the stinking succesh, General. I said, Goodnight. You'll take a turn with me nonetheless, Bessie?

ELIZABETH: I should say not.

GRANT: Well, you took a turn with him and we don't know who the hell he is!

ELIZABETH: All right, then, General, once around and then home you go.

HARRY: I wouldn't, Bessie. Not while Mr Grant is squiffed.

GRANT: Ah, fiddlesticks, Johnnie Reb. You get all the rest of the dances with her.

ELIZABETH: And you might, too, Mister Lehr.

(ELIZABETH *takes up a waltz with* GRANT.)

ELIZABETH: You have let me down, sir. But I am feeling half-crazy myself tonight.

GRANT: *(Dancing like Astaire)* I know, I know, I know. My word, what fun it is sometimes to be completely worthless!

ACT ONE   19

(HARRY *lights a cigar, watching, as* GRANT *and* ELIZABETH *whirl around.)*

Scene Five

(A table at Delmonico's. MRS FISH *is sitting with* MRS CAROLINE ASTOR.*)*

MRS ASTOR: So Harry is bringing his belle around for lunch?

MRS FISH: Very important. Very important she like us. Very important we like her, and if we don't like her, very important we lie with all our customary grace.

MRS ASTOR: It would be sad if things didn't turn out well for him.

MRS FISH: But we don't own him, Caroline.

MRS ASTOR: Oh, yes, yes, I think we do. And, Mamie, I hope you will have some behavior about you.

MRS FISH: Whenever have I not?

MRS ASTOR: Well, to take one example, my sister-in-law is very cross with you just now. She heard how you told some people that she looked like a frog.

MRS FISH: Then, when you see her again, say she got it wrong. What I said was toad. She looks just like a toad.

MRS ASTOR: I could never repeat that.

MRS FISH: No, I suppose you couldn't. You have many millions at your disposal and I have just a few.

MRS ASTOR: You see? You are doing it again!

MRS FISH: You can read and write, in several languages. I can barely read or write in my own. You have a dignity, I have a flair.

MRS ASTOR: You could have your dignity, too, you know, if you tried a little harder.

MRS FISH: I doubt it. In fact, I think the world needs both of us. But, still, we will always revere you, Mrs Astor. *The* Mrs Astor.

MRS ASTOR: I *have* labored mightily to introduce some order into the world of privilege.

MRS FISH: Because only four hundred people can fit into your ballroom. I can fit forty, at most, in mine, and even then, they are too many. Four is about right. But we all revere you. Still, you don't know most of us that well and you never really talk to us, the Four Hundred or so, but we are all constrained to revere you nonetheless.

MRS ASTOR: Then would you kindly begin the revering now by not talking about this anymore?

MRS FISH: No. Because someone asked me a question recently that he would never dare ask you, because he revered you. He asked me, Just how *large*, finally, Mrs Fish, is your social standing?

MRS ASTOR: Really? That's quite rude. And what did you answer?

MRS FISH: I said, I can't tell you, because it swells at night.

MRS ASTOR: *(Looking off)* Oh, my, they're here. Now, Mamie, please, no more smutty talk.

(ELIZABETH *and* HARRY *approach.*)

HARRY: My dear friends, it is my sacred pleasure to make this introduction. Mrs Mary Grace Anthon Stuyvesant Fish, Mrs Caroline Astor, this is Mrs Elizabeth Drexel Dahlgren.

MRS ASTOR: How do you do, Mrs Dahlgren?

MRS FISH: *Enchanté.* No, really, I know that sounds hopeless, but I am really quite *enchanté. Enchanté* to the gills.

ACT ONE 21

ELIZABETH: It is an honor to meet you. Harry speaks of you both so very highly.

MRS FISH: I'm sure he does. Highly and, in my case, lowly. And we don't mean to put you on the spot, but…what is your favorite flower?

ELIZABETH: Flower?

MRS FISH: One can tell so much from horticultural analogies.

ELIZABETH: Well, I suppose I favor the lily.

MRS FISH: That is so sweet. Isn't that sweet, Caroline? Lilies have such a holy sound about them.

MRS ASTOR: I prefer the snapdragon.

MRS FISH: I should think you would.

HARRY: And we all know what your favorite is, my pet. The climbing rose, is it not?

MRS FISH: And yours—the marry-gold?

ELIZABETH: I must say, Harry, your friends all talk so smart, I'm at a loss.

MRS ASTOR: Please, don't be. Mrs Fish is desperate to find authentic people, that is, people she would consider to be authentic.

ELIZABETH: And you're not?

MRS ASTOR: I don't search people out, as a rule.

MRS FISH: As a rule, they search her out. But, lookee here, Mrs Dahlgren…

ELIZABETH: Bessie, if you like.

MRS FISH: Oh, certainly, Bessie if I like. I'm Mamie, if you like or don't. But you can't call the old snapdragon here "Carrie." She hates familiarity.

MRS ASTOR: *(Trying to gets things to center)* Mrs Dahlgren—Bessie, if you would. I understand how under the light you must feel. Harry has many friends and they all treasure him dearly, as, it is possible, we may come to treasure you as well. And we are all women, Harry's good friends, so we exercise a certain outrageous prerogative to know better what happens to him.

ELIZABETH: I have no idea what will happen to him. I thought we were going to have a simple lunch, as Mr Lehr told me on the way here.

MRS FISH: What Caroline means to say, in her solemn and ham-fisted way, is that we are predisposed to like you because old Harry here likes you. And it is not as though we don't know a little here and there—I mean, the Drexels of Philadelphia were always to be reckoned with, good money, solid money, honest money. And the breeding.

ELIZABETH: We would like to think so. We would also like to think—with your permission—that what we make of our opportunities in this world will be just exactly what we bring with us inwardly, where our souls are said to dwell, so that if, some fine day, we were stripped of all our outer forms, we would carry ourselves with the same virtue and dignity.

HARRY: Of course.

MRS FISH: Well said.

MRS ASTOR: Yes, I do see your position. But we can never ever behave as though it were possible for us to be…reduced. We are not people who can be reduced. We are, in so many ways, chosen.

ELIZABETH: I'm not sure that I agree with you, Mrs Astor.

MRS ASTOR: You needn't. You're young. In time, the responsibilities of being a leader will come to you in ways you can hardly imagine.

ACT ONE

ELIZABETH: I never expect to lead anything.

MRS FISH: Well, don't just follow, for God's sake. Don't just wander behind and bleat.

ELIZABETH: No. I don't expect that either. I do intend to find the means to be the equal of such distinguished women as yourselves, but in my own way. *(Suddenly taking his hand)* Really, Harry, I'm not sure I can explain all these things to your friends, who have seen and done so much. *(Gets up)* If you will allow me a moment, I will compose myself a little more exactly. *(Helpless)* Dear Mister Lehr… *(Exits)*

MRS FISH: Well…

HARRY: Well…?

MRS ASTOR: I can't speak for the two of you, but I like her. I like her a good deal.

MRS FISH: So do I. Harry?

HARRY: She arrived on my arm, she'll leave on my arm. Is there anything else I can tell you?

MRS FISH: I think we shall be able to make something of her. In fact, we are going to make the world of her, and you.

MRS ASTOR: Yes, Harry, she is acceptable to me. *(Standing)* I've been here much too long. Please give her…Mrs Dahlgren…my apologies and ask her to call on me. I hope, as time goes by, that she will bring us all closer together and not the other way around. That is what I sincerely hope. *(Exits)*

MRS FISH: Well, Jesus wept, Harry. You did something right.

HARRY: I hope. All I've wanted these recent days is to make a little more regular place for myself in society.

MRS FISH: I know you've also wanted, pretty plainly, to stand outside, with me at your side, and laugh your damn-fool head off.

HARRY: But you have a home, you have a husband, you have children. Whatever they say about us after all, you have upheld all the virtues by which we finally shall be judged. I think I better throw myself into it, too.

MRS FISH: Throw yourself into nothing but a magnum of champagne. I am an ugly and useless person with pots of money. You are a handsome and useful person without a red cent.

HARRY: *Nous nous soutenons.*

MRS FISH: We stand by each other, and always shall.

HARRY: I guess I should drink to that.

MRS FISH: You bloody well better, if you know what's good for you!

(HARRY *and* MRS FISH *hoist their glasses.*)

(*Blackout*)

Scene Six

(HARRY's *apartment at the Waldorf. He is dressing slowly, and* JOHNNIE *is helping him.*)

JOHNNIE: How did you suddenly grow all these thumbs, mister?

HARRY: I'm a little nervous today.

JOHNNIE: And why would that be?

HARRY: Because I'll be entertaining at home. Entertaining, that is, this very special woman I have met.

ACT ONE

JOHNNIE: You sure you hadn't better take another brandy, then?

HARRY: No. I want to be alert to everything. *(Admiring himself)* What do you think of us, Johnnie?

JOHNNIE: Us? I don't know nothin' of any "us." I think different of me than of you.

HARRY: All right. What do you think of me?

JOHNNIE: No, sir. I ain't gonna do that. Some things I observe are strictly for my own delectation, late at night, when I'm with my own.

HARRY: You're not afraid of your employment, are you?

JOHNNIE: I don't think so. If you was run down by a trolley car tomorrow and the injury was to be mortal, the which, of course, I don't hope, there's four or five places already offered me assorted venues at considerably more spendable currency than I get from you.

HARRY: So? How can it harm to tell me what you think? Frankly, I need an honest word here.

JOHNNIE: I value being in your company, is all. Also, contrary to all my good sense, which was born and bred into me in a sizeable amount by my own folks, who themselves used to be owned by other white people not unlike yourself, I believe I've come to like you.

HARRY: For God's sake, man, that's what I'm asking—why?

JOHNNIE: Look at the lilies of the field, sir. They toil not, neither do they spin. Yet Solomon, in all his glory, was not so sweetly arrayed as one of them…or yourself, on a good day.

HARRY: You mean I am a dress dummy?

JOHNNIE: I mean, you are the exact picture of the time and the place over which you reign supreme, like a conqueror. Now, ain't that enough?

HARRY: That's what I wonder. You know who I really am, Johnnie. And, Johnnie, you know that usually I envy no one. Today, Johnnie, I envy the whole world. Even you, Johnnie.

JOHNNIE: Well, thank you for the time of day.

HARRY: No. That's why I watch you so closely. You always give yourself the choice of getting out of this little bubble whenever you want.

JOHNNIE: You might say I don't need what you need to survive.

HARRY: You need every bit as much.

JOHNNIE: Well, I surely don't need to walk one way when the sun shines, and another way in the darker places at midnight.

HARRY: *(Suddenly not* JOHNNIE's *friend anymore)* I'm sorry you mentioned that.

JOHNNIE: You asked.

HARRY: You will never mention it again. I do, after all, love you. Don't make me have to destroy you.

(JOHNNIE *is about to lose his composure, too, when there is a knock at the door.)*

JOHNNIE: Let me do this, sir. It looks very impressive you got a servant, which is all I am, after all, to do your greetings.

(JOHNNIE *shows* ELIZABETH *in.)*

HARRY: Bessie, my dear.

ELIZABETH: Good afternoon, Harry.

HARRY: That's all for now, John.

ACT ONE

JOHNNIE: Very good, sir. (*Exits*)

ELIZABETH: These must be the nicest accommodations in the hotel.

HARRY: They are. They've been given to me.

ELIZABETH: Is that so? Someone must think you are a very important man.

HARRY: Someone does. In fact, a lot of someones think I'm very important. You've probably wondered once in a while how it is I make my living.

ELIZABETH: Quite a few questions *have* been asked, but I dismissed them, since I feel it is none of my business and ought to be none of anyone else's.

HARRY: I have many rich and famous friends. Consequently, the owner of the hotel lets me have this suite of rooms for no charge, because he knows I will tell my rich and famous friends about his kindness, and the rich and famous friends will come here to eat and drink and board their rich and famous guests. Another man gives me my suits, on condition I mention his establishment. Another man gives me my linen, on the same condition. Another man, my wines; another, my jewelry; another my pajamas, even. Mrs Astor believes I should be able to send anything I want anywhere I want at anytime, so I have free privileges at her husband's Western Union. Mrs Fish thinks I should be able to travel, so the Illinois and Grand Central Railroads have issued me passes. And if I want for folding money, it is Mister Ivan Kessler, the champagne vender, who provides me with six thousand dollars in cash each year to recommend his wares to people who claim they hate champagne, yet end up with a cellar full of his expensive bubbly. In short, for the past two years, I have not had to pay for a single expense I have run up.

ELIZABETH: You have such power?

HARRY: Limitless. But I am a poor man.

ELIZABETH: I don't see how you can say so.

HARRY: Nothing I have belongs to me. See here, Bessie, you have been able to make out, I hope, almost since our first meeting, that I have been quite taken with you—

ELIZABETH: But—

HARRY: Please. I also know that you are lonely, and that you need someone to watch over you and lead you through this sometimes-cruel society I understand so well. And I believe, I deeply believe, I am the man to help you do it. If, that is, I have not spoken out of turn.

ELIZABETH: Harry, I...

HARRY: What, my dearest?

ELIZABETH: How could you ever think—if you have any sense in your head at all—that I have not been drawn to you and waited on you and found delight in your presence?

HARRY: I have nothing to offer you in return.

ELIZABETH: That's not true. Through all the recent days and nights, you have been my guide, my mentor, my hero, my friend. Why would you make less of that?

HARRY: Because of my poverty. *(Pause)* Also, I am terribly afraid of what they call "romantic love."

ELIZABETH: I am the same way. Now I want very little to do with things that I consider to be low and bestial and not worthy of men and women who are made in God's image, as I believe we are, both of us, created in that form that holds so much to a beautiful respect and not an ugly passion. *(Pause)* So? What do you think of *that*, Mister Lehr?

ACT ONE

HARRY: *(Rings a little bell)* I think now we ought to have some tea, or even something a little stronger, to celebrate.

JOHNNIE: *(Entering)* Sir?

HARRY: Bring the refreshments, and you might uncork the champagne, the good stuff, that I had the people downstairs put on ice.

JOHNNIE: Yes, sir. *(Exits)*

ELIZABETH: Dear me. What are we celebrating again?

HARRY: That you and I admire each other so deeply.

ELIZABETH: I think we are talking about a marriage here, too, are we not? I mean, if it is acceptable that the woman raise the subject first.

HARRY: Yes, we might well be talking about a marriage, something I thought I would never do…

ELIZABETH: Something I thought I would never do again. But, let me ask you, first—are we in love?

HARRY: I'm damned if I know. I don't think so.

ELIZABETH: I don't think so, either. But I am so jealous of your company that I would do almost anything to insure it for the rest of my life.

HARRY: *(Taking her hand)* I feel the same way, exactly. But, now, what will this be about?

ELIZABETH: Whatever we want it to be about. A kind of life, Harry, that others will recognize as unique….

HARRY: That they will want to watch….

ELIZABETH: Yes, will want to watch in order to observe us….

HARRY: Together, in a more perfect union…

ELIZABETH: Free of grotesque behavior…

HARRY: An ideal state…

ELIZABETH: In which we help each other become larger, fuller, more free!

HARRY: Just think. Together, we might put their eye out.

ELIZABETH: Mightn't we just!

(JOHNNIE *pops in.*)

JOHNNIE: You'll pardon if this is a bad moment, sir. Did you say, again, the good stuff, or the very good stuff?

HARRY: The best stuff.

JOHNNIE: Yessir! *(Exits)*

HARRY: May I say one other thing, then?

ELIZABETH: Please, Harry.

HARRY: Once I am married, my sources, who value me most as this glamorous bird, the unmarried man, will dry up.

ELIZABETH: You mean you will need an income?

HARRY: I will have to find some sort of employment, yes, probably with a small banking firm, and it won't pay much at first.

ELIZABETH: But I have money.

HARRY: You need to hold on to what you have.

ELIZABETH: No. There is too much of it, it is not making me happy and it is not making anyone else happy, either. You could easily have twenty-five thousand dollars a year to live as you have. That would be right, wouldn't it, twenty-five thousand, to continue your good work of pleasing others?

HARRY: I couldn't let you.

ELIZABETH: No, I am sure it is the sensible solution. That way I know we shall always be friends, we shall always be close.

HARRY: And the "rapture" you told me you had never known in your life?

ELIZABETH: Oh, we two shall find it. I have no doubt of that. At the moment, however, we have struck our more modest bargain and so—may I borrow the loan of a kiss on it?

HARRY: With generous terms of repayment.

ELIZABETH: I expect no less.

(But, before ELIZABETH *and* HARRY *can,* JOHNNIE *enters with a big tray.)*

JOHNNIE: Sir, you'll excuse me again, I presume, but I get the feel of some little joy and hope in this otherwise usually dreary little room. Could I be wrong? *(As he opens the champagne, singing)*
There's a golden harp up in heaven for me,
There's a golden harp up in heaven for me,
There's a golden harp up in heaven for me,
'Cause I ain't gonna be here much longer!

(The champagne has been poured around and HARRY *offers* JOHNNIE *a glass as well.)*

ELIZABETH, HARRY & JOHNNY: *(Singing)*
You just pluck one string and the whole heavens ring,
You just pluck one string and the whole heavens ring,
You just pluck one string and the whole heavens ring,
'Cause I ain't gonna be here much longer!

(Blackout)

Scene Seven

(Portico of Saint Patrick's Cathedral. GRANT *stands watching the rain in a morning suit and tophat, smoking a cigar.* JOHNNIE *enters, under an umbrella, and takes shelter.)*

JOHNNIE: What a great day for a wedding at the Cathedral of the Saintly Patrick! *(Recognizing* GRANT*)* Ah, well, I see! A most distinguished guest. Let me introduce myself. I am the groom's, that is, Mister Harry Lehr's, body servant, I suppose you'd call me. John Goodenough is the name.

GRANT: *(Shaking hands very formally)* Mister Goodenough.

JOHNNIE: Johnnie is good enough for me. It's a wonderful morning, would you say, Mister President?

GRANT: Not anymore.

JOHNNIE: Because of the rain, sir?

GRANT: Because of the other part. I'm no longer the president.

JOHNNIE: Oh, well, I think you get to keep the title. You get to keep the title of General-Of-The-Armies, too, at least as far as I'm concerned.

GRANT: I used simply to be Mister Grant. Of course, things didn't work out so well for me when I was simply Mister Grant, but I do miss the young man who was called that. *(Bites down on his cigar; in pain)* Great God almighty! *(Throws the cigar away and holds his face a moment)*

JOHNNIE: You're not feeling well, sir?

GRANT: I don't know. Maybe I am, Johnnie, maybe I'm not. Somebody else will have to tell me.

ACT ONE 33

JOHNNIE: *(Producing a silver flask)* Would you like a little brandy?

(GRANT *hesitates.)*

JOHNNIE: Aw, g'won, sir, have some. Mister Lehr says I should always carry this, in case of snakes. I told him, there aren't no snakes in New York City. He says, You just don't see them, that's all. Well, right now, I do, there—across the street.

GRANT: Ah, yes, the surging crowds. All admirers of Mister Lehr, I take it, and not those of my dear Bessie. She rides today on his coattails, as I did on Mister Lincoln's. *(Pain again)* Jeezus! I don't know about this!

JOHNNIE: The brandy won't hurt, I promise.

GRANT: If you say so. *(Takes a healthy swig)* I see a faint smile on your lips there, Johnnie. Grant never said no to a drink, did he? Well, Grant has in the past, and Grant will again. Just Grant won't this moment, that's all, not in the teeth of the surging snakes.

JOHNNIE: Yes, sir.

GRANT: *(Another sip)* Grant was always very good when Grant knew Grant had a job to do. That's what the war was about, by the way. Despite what you've heard, about preserving the Union and freeing the slaves, with all deference to you, of course, the war was really about getting Grant a job he could manage finally, a job he was capable of, to keep him out of trouble. And there were some extremely memorable days laid end on end, when the fate of the nation hung in the balance, as they liked to describe it in the news dispatches back then. And Grant was not only very good, he was brilliant. Then there were all the other days, when nothing happened at all, and that's when you would find Grant in his tent, smoking and drinking and trying to do what he called mental balancing. "Brooding" might have been the better word, had Grant dared to use it.

JOHNNIE: Brooding about what?

GRANT: Grant didn't know, or he wouldn't have brooded. *(One more sip and he hands the flask back.)*

JOHNNIE: If you don't mind my offering something, Mister General-President, since we seem to be talking now as though we'd known each other all our lives—

GRANT: Say what you like, Johnnie. I am past social niceties.

JOHNNIE: I was thinking of the advantages. My Mister Harry and your Miss Elizabeth, they certainly do have a lot of the advantages.

GRANT: Indeed. And you'd like their advantages?

JOHNNIE: I'd like some of them. Some of them I could do without. To me, in the mood I've come to, I think these better sorts simply got a lot of time on their hands—Grant might say, between the battles—when they don't seem to do much of anything except brood.

GRANT: About money, most of them. That's young Mr Lehr's game, at any rate.

JOHNNIE: Well, sir—the money is the freedom. It is the power.

GRANT: I wouldn't know. I've made some in my life, been given some more, but I've also managed, one way or another, to lose every nickel I ever had.

JOHNNIE: But at least you had the taste of it. And always the opportunity to taste some more. And it seems to me that sooner or later, some of us, people like me, I mean, who come from a background of enslavement, are gonna want to take back some of what they believe was stolen off their enslaved work and their enslaved hopes. So I wonder, should we wait

ACT ONE 35

for what is due us, or should we find a way, cause nothing else seems to be happening, to steal it back again?

GRANT: I have no idea in the world. If you wait, it may never come. If you steal it, you're no better than they were and, for that matter, still are. And if you work harder than they do, it may never be recognized, let alone make a difference.

JOHNNIE: That's your answer?

GRANT: It's the best I can do. Your sort and my sort, despite the blood we've all let, may never find a way to live together.

JOHNNIE: Hell, I don't want to live with you—with all due respect. I don't even want to be anywhere near you for long. I just want what you got.

GRANT: *(Patting his pockets)* And here I was—going to see if I could borrow a dollar from you. *(Looking out)* Hold onto your seat, Johnnie! The crowd is edging forward, some of them hysterical.

JOHNNIE: I believe the bride's carriage just pulled up yonder, is the cause for the outbreak. They need a closer look at her.

GRANT: *(Straightening his tie)* Damned if you aren't right. My dearest Bessie...

JOHNNIE: Pretty as a picture. *(Pause)* I don't know, this minute, if I can say to you in proper speech what I mean. You see, I don't get to stand in the rain with many great men, like yourself. But it has been the pleasure of my lifetime to shake your hand and visit with you, despite that you have to be so filled with the gloomiest of doubts.

GRANT: Well, thank you, thank you very much. I take no special joy in knowing myself, but knowing you has done me a world of good as well. Do you suppose

I could have that flask again? I am beginning to see snakes everywhere.

(JOHNNIE *hands it to him;* GRANT *drinks.* ELIZABETH *appears, under a fancy parasol and in a beautiful wedding dress. The flask quickly disappears.*)

ELIZABETH: General...thank goodness, a friendly face. Johnnie, I think the groom will be wanting you.

JOHNNIE: Yes, ma'am. *(Tips his hat and exits)*

ELIZABETH: So, are you ready to give me away?

GRANT: It sounds bad when you put it like that, but I think I can do it. After all, what's involved? I take you so far, my heart aching a little, I hand you off to that fellah, you disappear with that fellah, I go home.

ELIZABETH: It may be more complicated.

GRANT: Oh, yes? I am obliged to go on the honeymoon as well?

ELIZABETH: No.

GRANT: You aren't having second thoughts, are you? Because the man who is going to give you away with a smile on his face, is the wrong man to tell.

ELIZABETH: You don't like Harry, do you?

GRANT: Like him? I barely know him. I know his type, though, because we had them hanging around the camps during the war. Not soldiers and not civilians, even. Ostlers, some called them. Subtlers, they called themselves. Merchants. They sold the men everything they needed that they couldn't get, and sold it at a price that would've made your hair stand on end. They were all very charming, very fast on their feet, and every one said he was your special friend.

ELIZABETH: I know what the dangers are, General. I am not young. I wasn't born young. And it could be, perhaps, like your soldier boys, I am a long way from

ACT ONE

home, very afraid of dying without ever having lived, and needing whatever hope I can buy.

GRANT: *(Moved)* Have you become so cynical, my dear?

ELIZABETH: Very much the contrary. Harry is not an ostler or a subtler. He's a good man, a decent man, a spiritual man who has consented to be my companion for the rest of my life.

GRANT: Good. Just make sure he doesn't overcharge you.

ELIZABETH: You know, you are being terribly wicked. Let me smell your breath. Have you been drinking? You've been drinking, haven't you?

GRANT: I had a brandy.

ELIZABETH: Oh, really!

GRANT: Don't go on about it. The colored fellah gave it to me. It eased the pain.

ELIZABETH: What pain?

GRANT: I was having breakfast the other morning and I bit into an orange. It hit something in my mouth—the tooth, the gum, I don't know—and it went right up through my head like a spike.

ELIZABETH: Then you should have it taken care of. And no more cigars.

GRANT: No more cigars. Elizabeth, you seem to me just now so very, very undefended, I want to pick up my sword again.

ELIZABETH: Thank you for the offer, but I can jolly well take care of myself.

GRANT: Good luck. *(Pause)* I mean that, by the way.

(ELIZABETH *kisses* GRANT *on the cheek. Strains of the Wedding March from "Lohengrin" are heard in the church.*)

GRANT: I believe that means we're being mustered. *(Takes her arm)*

ELIZABETH: Dear General, it is as though I were starting again, and my heart is beating very fast.

GRANT: As well it ought to. The world, if you tread very carefully, is at your feet.

(As ELIZABETH and GRANT turn and enter the church...)

(Blackout)

Scene Eight

(Smoky parlor car of a fast-moving train. A few shadowy figures drink as JOHNNIE bangs a spoon on a glass for attention.)

JOHNNIE: Gentlemen, at the special request of some of you Southerners who knew her a way back when—and I do mean, a way back, though just when, I'm not sure—it is my peculiar honor to present, for the last time on this or any other railroad hurtling posthaste to Baltimore, Maryland, that gemstone too long out of her setting and never to be laid in that setting again, Atlanta's favorite and only true belle, the Lady herself!

(Applause and whistles as HARRY, in his wife's wedding dress, appears. JOHNNIE plucks out the accompaniment on a banjo, someone beats the rhythm on a table and HARRY sings with feeling.)

HARRY: So, you're going away
Because your heart has gone astray,
And you promised me
That you would always faithful be.

Go to him you love,
And be as true as stars above;
But your heart will still yearn,
And then someday you will return.

ACT ONE

Goodbye, my lady love,
Farewell, my turtle dove,
You are the idol and darling of my heart,
But someday you will come back to me,
And love me tenderly,
So, goodbye, my lady love, goodbye!

When the dewdrops fall,
'Tis your heart, I know, will call.
So beware, my dove,
Don't trust your life to some false love.

But if you must go,
Remember, dear, I love you so,
Sure as stars do shine,
You'll think of when I called you mine.

Goodbye, my lady love,
Farewell, my turtle dove,
You are the idol and darling of my heart,
But someday you will come back to me,
And love me tenderly,
So, goodbye, my lady love, goodbye!

(On the final few phrases, ELIZABETH, *in traveling clothes, has wandered in and watches. At the very end,* HARRY *pulls off his wig to wild applause.)*

ELIZABETH: *(Not angry)* Harry, is that really you!

GENTLEMAN: No ladies allowed in here, ma'am.

ELIZABETH: Dear Harry!

(Blackout)

Scene Nine

(Sitting room of a hotel suite. ELIZABETH *enters in her travel clothes, followed by* JOHNNIE, *who is struggling with several big suitcases, which he puts down. As she takes off her coat, she looks at a table set for two.)*

ELIZABETH: They've done just fine, exactly what I asked for. Caviar. Quail in aspic. Champagne. His favorite cigars, his favorite roses.

JOHNNIE: It looks very nice, ma'am.

ELIZABETH: A modest, but luxuriant, wedding repast. You'd better go see about Mister Lehr now.

JOHNNIE: Yes, ma'am.

ELIZABETH: *(As* JOHNNIE *is going)* You've known your employer a long while now, John. I haven't. I never knew he was a theatrical impersonator.

JOHNNIE: Oh, well, that's something he did in the old days, when he was very poor and completely unknown. Lots of those people back then dressed up like the ladies, and his doing so brought him the attention he needed to get into this kind of social world. You surely don't think it was bad of him, do you?

ELIZABETH: Oh, no. I envy him his grace and his talent and his beauty. He certainly would have made a beautiful woman.

JOHNNIE: You think so? I think he'd of made an ugly woman.

ELIZABETH: Well, it's a moot question, isn't it? Now, would you tell him, please, that the table is set and I look forward to seeing him *toute suite*.

JOHNNIE: Yes, ma'am.

ACT ONE 41

(JOHNNIE *exits.* ELIZABETH *takes her diary from her purse and sits at the table, writing.*)

ELIZABETH: "I barely remember a moment of the day, except the General's illness, which must be taken care of"—Reminder to Bessie to bring this up with Harry—"and Harry's whispering to me, as we knelt at the altar of the great cathedral, `You are more lovely this moment than you have ever been and now God knows it, too, because He sees especially well in here.' I also do recall that my mother wept. She clutched me and said, `At last, one of my children is happy.' `Dear Mama,' I wanted to say, `this is not about being happy, but I have dared to hope.' I wonder which of us—Harry or me—will be the first to utter the word `love?'"

(JOHNNIE *knocks and then enters.*)

JOHNNIE: I beg your pardon, ma'am. Mister Lehr wishes me to inform you that he has ordered his food from downstairs and will be having his supper in his own room.

ELIZABETH: Well, that must be a mistake. Would you be so good as to confirm that you heard his message correctly?

JOHNNIE: Yes, ma'am. *(Exits)*

ELIZABETH: *(Picks up her diary again, deeply puzzled, and writes)* "Baltimore is very different than New York...." *(Scribbles it out)* "Baltimore is very different from New York. There are no legions of the poor teeming through the streets..." *(Scribbles it out)* "There are no poor people to be seen, only the well born and comfortable..." *(Scribbles it out)* "No....no....no...."

(HARRY *knocks and enters.* ELIZABETH *quickly hides her diary.*)

ELIZABETH: *(Tries to approach him)* Harry, dearest...?

HARRY: *(Backing off)* I'm sorry. I'm afraid this is the way things must be.

ELIZABETH: What things?

HARRY: Tonight, I will have my meal alone. And all the nights in the future as well, when we are not out in public.

ELIZABETH: Whyever on earth?

HARRY: We both knew, when we began, and agreed upon it absolutely, that we would never be caught up in the common farce of romance and sentiment.

ELIZABETH: Yes, but Harry, this is just a meal.

HARRY: It is more than a meal. It is a way of life neither of us can profitably subscribe to.

ELIZABETH: Simply to break bread together?

HARRY: Yes. After the meal, you would probably want me to sit with you, even into the late hours. And thereafter, you would doubtless expect me to share your bed.

ELIZABETH: Not my bed. Our bed.

HARRY: But, you see, I'm telling you now, here, firmly and finally, there can never be such as thing as our bed.

ELIZABETH: This is not right, Harry.

HARRY: How many men, men who are husbands of friends of yours, have entered their boudoirs on the wedding night in the same state of mind as myself and gone through with something that was both terrible and false. Have you ever asked yourself, what did they want?

ELIZABETH: Well, what *did* they want? What did *you* want?

ACT ONE

HARRY: Nothing more than to care for you as we agreed and be by myself when I choose. I prefer the truth, as difficult as it may be, to hypocrisy.

ELIZABETH: So, given some time, time that will pass quickly, for me, for you…

HARRY: No. This is the way it will always be. May I say again, I am sorry. I am so sorry you didn't understand. I thought our bargain was very clear. From you, I would get money and a decent social position. From me, you would—and will—get the kind of celebrity most women in the upper ranks only dream of.

ELIZABETH: I truly believed you had some feelings toward me that ran a little deeper.

HARRY: Oh, I have feelings. My God, do I have feelings. If I were ever to love anyone in this life, it would be you.

ELIZABETH: So, this is the "more perfect union" we talked up so heartily?

HARRY: Yes.

ELIZABETH: How can it be called a union unless we are united in everything?

HARRY: *(Sincerely)* Please, Elizabeth. I am suddenly very afraid.

ELIZABETH: Of me?

HARRY: Of myself.

ELIZABETH: So, because of that, I am to be even more alone than I was before I met you.

HARRY: No.

ELIZABETH: That is how you have just made me feel.

HARRY: Please don't try to work on sympathies I probably don't have. When you write about it in your diary, which I know you will do, write it down thusly—that you married a man who turned out to be like one of those men in the novels written for women, a man who is an opportunist, who lives off rich ladies, who has no morals at all, but who brought gaiety and charm and color and excitement to their lives.

ELIZABETH: You cannot not just suddenly become all of that.

HARRY: Write it down as so. Know it to be true. But remember—and this is my solemn promise—I will never be anything but adoring and attentive toward you when we are out before the world.

ELIZABETH: But here, between ourselves…?

HARRY: As I said, respectful but apart.

ELIZABETH: This is unacceptable to me.

HARRY: You have no choice now. You've but to think of your mother, who counts on you for her very survival. This is her marriage, too.

ELIZABETH: You have me, now, is that it? And so you can be a bastard.

HARRY: *(Suddenly puts his arms around her and holds her tight)* Dear heart, have you looked at the kingdom we have inherited—the finest condition mankind has ever known: health, wealth without end, beautiful people as our adoring friends. And if we are so weak as to crave the baser pleasures, they can always be had on the side for a song.

ELIZABETH: *(Pulling away)* NO!

HARRY: YOU MUST NOT LET THIS HURT YOU!

ELIZABETH: BUT IT HAS!

HARRY: NO! WE ARE NOT THAT SORT OF PEOPLE! *(Recovering; kissing her hand)* Now we should get our new lives started with a well-deserved rest. Good night.

ACT ONE

ELIZABETH: Good night. *(Pause)* And goodbye.

HARRY: You needn't, really, make it sound so final.

(HARRY *exits.* ELIZABETH *pulls out her diary and clutches it. A knock and* JOHNNIE *comes in.*)

ELIZABETH: Yes, John?

JOHNNIE: I'm sorry, ma'am. Sorry about much of everything.

ELIZABETH: That's all right, John. I want to make some reservations for a railroad train to Philadelphia. If not tonight, then tomorrow morning.

JOHNNIE: I think I can do that.

ELIZABETH: The reservation will be for one.

JOHNNIE: Yes, ma'am.

ELIZABETH: For one, I said.

JOHNNIE: Yes, ma'am. Will there be a return trip?

ELIZABETH: I don't think so. *(Pause)* John, have you eaten since we arrived here?

JOHNNIE: No, ma'am.

ELIZABETH: Will you join me for dinner? The table is, after all, set for two.

JOHNNIE: This is Baltimore, ma'am. You'd not like it known much that you ate with a colored.

ELIZABETH: I'll tell them I hadn't noticed. Now, please. That is a formal request, the mistress to the servant.

JOHNNIE: Yes, ma'am.

(JOHNNIE *sits down.* ELIZABETH *pours champagne for both of them and raises a glass.*)

ELIZABETH: *(Singing)* Goodbye, my lady love,
Farewell, my turtle dove,
You are the idol and darling of my heart,
But someday you will come back to me,

And love me tenderly,
So, goodbye, my lady love, goodbye!

(Blackout)

END OF ACT ONE

ACT TWO

Scene One

(A huge lawn party in the background, under tents and lit by Chinese lanterns. Drum roll, scattered applause everywhere as JOHNNIE, *in swell clothes, takes his place on a small platform at an upright piano.)*

JOHNNIE: After all the fine amusements of a Rhode Island evening, and before your hostess, Mrs Stuyvesant Fish, has the orchestra play *her* favorite tune— *(As he does a little on the piano)* "Show Me The Way To Go Home"—That's how it always happens at her parties, isn't it?—there has been a request that a certain Mister Popular Bones, formerly of Atlanta, Georgia, and lately of somewhere on the Isle of Manhattan, favor us with a very contemporary melody. I know many of you were disappointed that the Crown Prince of All the Balkans couldn't make it to this shindig—the competition for His Royal Highness's highness was very fierce—but you all had a better time here, because you could bring your canine friends to the first ever "Dinner for Dogs" and they were served off the finest china, to boot. Mrs Fish is sending the caterers home—I can see her back there paying them off—so this best be quick. Ladies and gentlemen, here he is and he really is a one with all of you—Mister Harry—or should I be more regal, considering his word is the law in the principalities of the drawing room and the card room and the ballroom, not to

mention the powder room —the one and the only—
King Lehr!

(HARRY *appears in blackface and evening clothes,* JOHNNIE *pounds the piano, and* HARRY *tears into—*)

HARRY: When I was born they christened me plain Samuel Johnson Brown,
I hadn't grown so very big 'fore some folks in the town
Had changed it 'round to Sambo, I was Rastus to a few,
Then Chocolate Drop was added by some others that I knew
And then to cap the climax, I was strolling down the line
When someone shouted "fellers hey, come on and pipe the shine,"
But I don't care a bit....
Here's how I figure it:
'Cause my hair is curly,
'Cause my teeth are pearly,
Just because I always wear a smile,
Like to dress up in the latest style,
'Cause I'm glad I'm living.
Take trouble smiling, never whine,
Just because my color's shady,
Slightly different maybe,
That's why they call me "shine."

A rose, they say, by any other name would smell as sweet,
So if that's right why should a nickname take me off my feet,
Why ev'rything that's precious from a gold piece to a dime
And diamonds, pearls, and rubies ain't no good unless they shine,
So when these clever people call me shine or coon or smoke,
I simply smile and then smile some more and vote

them all a joke,
I'm thinking just the same…
What is there in a name?

'Cause my hair is curly,
'Cause my teeth are pearly,
Just because I always wear a smile,
Like to dress up in the latest style,
'Cause I'm glad I'm living.
Take trouble smiling, never whine,
Just because my color's shady,
Slightly different maybe,
That's why they call me "shine."

(At the very end, HARRY, at the peak of his form, holds the note too long, in a grand pose, and collapses on the platform. "Oohs," "Aaaahs," and a shriek.)

(Blackout)

Scene Two

(Afterwards, at the same party. HARRY is propped up in a chair, being fanned by JOHNNIE. MRS FISH sits at his table, as does ELIZABETH, who says nothing.)

MRS FISH: Now the bejewelled mob has gone, I can catch my breath. Did you see Caroline Astor? So many diamonds wrapped around her in this summer heat, she looked like a chandelier. Are you sure you're okay, Harry?

HARRY: Yes, my pet, much better. The applause of our guests picked up my spirits immeasurably. Johnnie, my boy, see to the kitchen and have them bring me a glass of milk and a hard-boiled egg.

JOHNNIE: Yes, sir. *(Exits)*

MRS FISH: *(Holding a news clip)* Here's something that will make you feel better as well. From the Newport

Morning Telegraph… *(Reads operatically through her lorgnette)* "The seaside Valhalla of swaggerdom is dull—dull as a Presidential message, or a Punch joke. But what cares Newport? It can console itself with its new bona fide sensation—Harry Lehr's laugh."

(HARRY *laughs.*)

MRS FISH: "The jaded souls of Newport's 'h'inner suckles' seem acted upon by this new and potent stimulant. As society's court jester, Harry is a wonder. He has held up the town with his irresistible chuckle and robbed it of invitations to dinners, musicales, yacht cruises, barn dances and heaven knows what not, at his piratical pleasure!"

HARRY: But I fear we have not done enough, Mamie, to hold their attention.

MRS FISH: Or too much, perhaps, according to this other correspondent, who writes in the letters column that "certain people" —I believe she means you and I, Harry— "are holding society up to ridicule to such an extent that there might be a loss of respect amongst lesser people for great wealth and the privilege it brings."

HARRY: I know of the lady. Has a cheap cottage down at the end of the row. Her liver is inflamed with jealousy.

MRS FISH: Quite right. Now, I think, as the evening dew silvers the trampled-down grass blades, is the moment for one last glass of the grape. Is there any of the help still around?

(As MRS FISH *gets up and exits, same time and distantly,* GRANT *comes in, leaning on a cane, and escorted by* CHARLIE. *They stand a moment as* CHARLIE *helps* GRANT *light a cigar.)*

ACT TWO

HARRY: So, what do you have to say for yourself, Bessie? Did you like my little exhibition tonight?

ELIZABETH: I missed it, I'm afraid. Went walking down by the water. There's a full moon, did you take a moment to notice?

HARRY: I shook them up a bit with the darkie number.

ELIZABETH: I really don't know why you have to make fun of every last thing in the world.

HARRY: All I do is put on the faces of people I love but can never be. Where's the harm in that? *(Rising suddenly)* Oh, look, the whole gaggle of Vanderbilts is leaving. *(Waves at them)* Let's show them what it's all about.

(HARRY *claps an arm around* ELIZABETH *and holds her tightly as he continues waving.*)

ELIZABETH: *(Also waving)* Harry, I am returning to the city early. Tomorrow, in fact.

HARRY: But you can't. We have a full schedule of places to go and be seen at.

ELIZABETH: You do, Harry. I don't.

HARRY: Good lord, Bessie. Despite a rather rocky start, we've made a good show out of being married these past two years, and have I ever treated you badly?

ELIZABETH: Oh, my, no, never in public. Now let go of me.

HARRY: Only if you promise to stay.

ELIZABETH: No. You told me we could always go our separate ways in this whatever-you-want-to-call-it that we have, this matrimonial arrangement.

HARRY: But never just toddle off in different directions. It doesn't look good.

ELIZABETH: *(Breaking away from* HARRY*)* The hell with how it looks, Harry! The hell with it! *(Pause)* I'm sorry.

HARRY: I should think so.

ELIZABETH: This isn't easy for me, this kind of life we lead. And I am so ashamed that I cannot imagine a decent way out of it.

HARRY: *(Looking off; gently)* Shhh! Shhh! They're coming back. We'll put a face on it, shall we, and talk about it all later.

(JOHNNIE *and* MRS FISH *enter.)*

MRS FISH: Would you believe? The parched throngs soaked up all my champagne!

JOHNNIE: And they don't know nothin' in that kitchen about making no glass of milk nor hard-boiling no egg.

HARRY: The picture of our lives—pheasant, venison and crepes Suzette—and not a simple meal to be had. I'll see about this. *(Getting up)* Come along, Johnnie.

(HARRY *kisses* ELIZABETH *gently on the cheek and exits with* JOHNNIE. *At the same time,* GRANT *and* CHARLIE *stroll over.)*

ELIZABETH: General…?

GRANT: *(Sitting down)* I had such fun, Bessie, watching this crazy party from a chair they fixed for me over there.

ELIZABETH: Do you know Mrs Fish?

GRANT: Yes, I received the honor at the door. She said to me, I think, "What a pleasure to have you, Mister President, a genuine relic amongst the multitude of specious artifacts."

MRS FISH: I may have said that. In fact, I believe I did. It certainly sounds like me. I had already had several cocktails.

ACT TWO

ELIZABETH: You haven't introduced your guest.

GRANT: He's not really my guest. Just met him, in fact. His father was a good soldier and a dear friend of mine during the war's darkest hours, and I was the one had to write the letter home, telling of his untimely death on the field of battle.

ELIZABETH: How do you do, sir? I am Mrs Elizabeth Drexel Lehr and this is your—our—hostess, Mrs Stuyvesant Fish.

CHARLIE: How do you do? I am pleased to meet you.

MRS FISH: Mister…?

CHARLIE: Mister is fine with me. I am not on any of your lists, I'm afraid.

MRS FISH: Lists go fry. It takes no more than the common knowledge of today's regatta, in which you sailed with such distinction, to know that you are one of us. Make yourself right to home. *(Standing)* Mister President, as you say you are not feeling altogether well, on my sideboard is a concoction of my husband's that cures, or at least, alleviates most suffering. Would you join me, and, afterwards, we'll find a bed for you in this large, overpriced bawdy house that we rent from some absentee rag-and-bone merchant.

GRANT: *(Rising, also)* You are most kind.

ELIZABETH: *(Censorious)* General…

GRANT: No, no, no, Bessie. It's nothing. I'm going to watch her drink it. That way, I can share her relief at my suffering.

(MRS FISH *takes* GRANT's *arm and they exit.* CHARLIE *and* ELIZABETH *alone)*

ELIZABETH: So…Mister…?

CHARLIE: Why don't you just call me Charlie.

ELIZABETH: Do you live around here?

CHARLIE: I used to, a long time ago, when I was in short pants. Now I reside in the West.

ELIZABETH: I am interested in the West, too. Which part do you call home?

CHARLIE: Detroit. Which parts were you interested in?

ELIZABETH: All over. Anywhere, I guess. I visited Colorado once. But it seemed like the dark side of the moon. I have, however, dreamed of going a thousand other places in that wild country.

CHARLIE: Really? Are you so unhappy here?

ELIZABETH: I beg your pardon?

CHARLIE: I thought I saw something in your eyes, something a little careworn, a little defeated.

ELIZABETH: What you see in my eyes is what you want to see there.

CHARLIE: Then I beg your pardon. It could be that I have been away from the Eastern seaboard for too long now and I've lost the knack of reading the manners and morals. But you know, when I was a gallant youth and coming of age here, we didn't have all this present silliness where the men hide out in their clubs all day, drinking steadily, while their wives dress up in beads and spangles, and your husband, I take it, Mister Lehr, leads the parade.

ELIZABETH: All of us condemned in one fell swoop?

CHARLIE: No. Just you, in fact.

ELIZABETH: For someone who considers himself a gentleman and superior to the rest of us, you certainly do take liberties.

ACT TWO

CHARLIE: I don't live around here anymore, except to sail my father's old boat once in a while in the summer. So, I don't have to be nice.

ELIZABETH: I've met men like you before, outsiders with their sharp tongues and the good looks to go with it.

CHARLIE: How do you know I'm not different?

ELIZABETH: Because you have no real idea what purpose our lives might have.

CHARLIE: Do you?

ELIZABETH: I know far more than some adventurer who has turned his back on his roots and gone roving through the mountains and plains with feathers in his hair, if not in his head.

CHARLIE: Detroit is about machinery, not wilderness. Detroit is about the future.

ELIZABETH: Is it, then, my dear engineer? Well, I would like you to know that millions of people have lived lives far worse than we do, and though there may be some among us who indulge themselves a little, we are solid people, sir. In our daily sacrifices, we count for something.

CHARLIE: Good. Good for you. Keep sacrificing. Now I really must take my leave. I return home tomorrow, to the mountains and plains, as you put it, and probably won't see you soon again, if at all. Though, it has been my pleasure.

ELIZABETH: Well, it has not been mine.

CHARLIE: Sorry to hear that. But still, how much, in your heart of hearts, you must hate this, all of it. *(Exits)*

ELIZABETH: BUT I DON'T HATE IT, MR CHARLIE-WHOEVER-YOU-ARE! I DON'T!

(Blackout)

Scene Three

(At home, HARRY sits alone, drinking brandy and reading an opera program. JOHNNIE enters.)

JOHNNIE: Mister Lehr?

HARRY: Ah, hello there, Johnnie. You're always around somewhere, aren't you? Have a drink?

JOHNNIE: No, thank you, sir. *(Hands HARRY some papers)* From your creditors. The expenses this month are about enough to break the bank at Monte Carlo.

HARRY: *(Scanning them)* As usual, a miserable, rainy, damp day. Went to twelve o'clock Mass at Saint Patrick's. Nobody I knew was there. Came home and ate lunch alone and then went to "Rigoletto" at the Opera, and it was mediocre. The air was hot, the atmosphere awful. Nobody in the usual crowd even bothered to attend. Went for a walk, which I hate to do. Nobody I knew was out. Had a drink alone at Delmonico's. Nobody at the bar even nodded or smiled. *(Tossing aside the bills)* So…what's left of my day?

JOHNNIE: *(Takes out a notebook)* You have dinner with that cattle-baron family, the Johnsons of Texas. Mrs Astor is attending, much against her will, but she thinks new money needs watching. Then a pianoforte recital at Mrs Betsy Bingham's. Mrs Stuyvesant Fish asks especially that you be punctual. I think she has something in mind that involves a pig. She said.

HARRY: I am aware of all that, thank you. It's afterwards I'm concerned about.

JOHNNIE: Come home.

HARRY: You know I've never done that.

JOHNNIE: I know you had better.

HARRY: Why?

ACT TWO

JOHNNIE: A man from the *Herald-Tribune* offered me a very large sum of money to tell the truth about my inside information of you and your true life, the way maids and butlers all over the town make some spare change tattling. He felt it could bring about the Revolution. What sort of revolution, he didn't say. So, I punched him in the nose.

HARRY: A smart idea.

JOHNNIE: But I might not punch the next one.

HARRY: What difference does it make? What do you really know about me that could be worth anybody's money?

JOHNNIE: Nothing. But I suspect things. I never met two people like you and the Missus who were so famous and lovely together in public and didn't do nothing to home except keep out of each other's tracks. I know she don't love anybody else, because I can tell those things, but I also know you do have your kind of loving, at strange hours, in stranger places—men, women, even that raggamuffin news boy who hangs around in Astor Place.

HARRY: I look on him as the child I shall never have.

JOHNNIE: Well, that's all I have to say about that—because this conversation is making my feet very itchy to move on out of here.

HARRY: Sometimes I need to have you around.

JOHNNIE: Sometimes I don't want to be.

HARRY: I pay you well for your time.

JOHNNIE: Then be especially careful, would be my advice, and recall, as you're circumnavigating with me, that if I had all your advantages and were painted white like yourself, I wouldn't spend my time drinking and loitering with strangers and feeling bad about myself. No, sir, I'd be out to do something.

HARRY: Like what?

JOHNNIE: Change the world.

HARRY: Lucky you. I've forgotten everything about what I wanted when I embarked on this brilliant career of mine.

JOHNNIE: Including your beautiful missus?

HARRY: Oh, well, she's pretty damn well forgot what she wanted, too. Only you, Johnnie, of all the people I know, are clear.

JOHNNIE: Are you romancing me, sir?

HARRY: No. It wouldn't get me anywhere anyway, would it? And you'd find it one more reason to censure me.

JOHNNIE: Would it make you happy, then, if I told you that I think you are a bad man?

HARRY: An evil man?

JOHNNIE: No, sir. Just ordinary bad.

HARRY: You must be as in love with me as I am with you. It makes perfect sense. You and I are the same person—born with nothing in order to make a little something, only to die with less. Neither of us will ever be completely acceptable. We are brothers.

JOHNNIE: You don't want to be in my family. We got too much to do, and you're too lazy to fit.

HARRY: Then be lazy with me, you son-of-a-bitch! Together, we could light up the sky!

JOHNNIE: I'm afraid I'd break your neck first.

(ELIZABETH *comes in.*)

ELIZABETH: My, my, you men were making such a noise.

HARRY: Johnnie doesn't approve.

ELIZABETH: Of what?

HARRY: Of who I am.

JOHNNIE: "Will that be all, sir?" "Yes, that will be all, Johnnie." "Thank you, sir." "You're welcome, Johnnie. Now run along." And Johnnie, he ran along. *(Exits)*

ELIZABETH: Harry, I've had a letter from a man I met last summer in Newport who is suddenly in town for a brief visit. I'm going out to have tea with him.

HARRY: And he struck your fancy?

ELIZABETH: As a matter of fact, he insulted me.

HARRY: How you must have loved that. *(Picking up the bills)* Johnnie was playing major domo just now, Bessie. He was looking over my expenses. It seems, one more time, I've run up a few more bills than my allowance can cover.

ELIZABETH: Write the checks out, Harry, and I'll sign them when I get back.

HARRY: And that's all? Why do we do this? I mean, I know why I do this. But why do you?

ELIZABETH: *(Putting on her gloves)* I do "this," as you call it, because that's what's expected of me. Do you like that answer? It makes my mother happy and it makes everybody else happy and I've learned you were right—we can get by just fine. I have joined four different groups now, all of them doing good work for persons less fortunate than ourselves, and a friendly little club that requires me to read all the new novels, as they come out, and I quite like that, too. Everywhere I go these days, people of both sexes treat with me with kindness, courtesy, and, sometimes, a little fear, because they know a word from me in your ear could alter their social fortunes. It's just as you said it would be, in fact: I've become a glittering prize—the celebrated wife of the much-more-celebrated Harry Lehr. Do you like that answer, also?

HARRY: Now you are making me jealous. I mean, I don't think I could live without you.

ELIZABETH: You had better knock on wood when you say that. It's been a slow closing of my life married to you, Harry. It makes the General's illness seem like the winking of an eye.

HARRY: Well, he hasn't long, has he?

ELIZABETH: No, he hasn't, and we appear to have forever. So let's both make something out of it, shall we?

HARRY: *(Suddenly embraces her)* I love you.

ELIZABETH: You don't!

HARRY: But I do.

ELIZABETH: *(Putting her arms around him)* Oh, dear God in heaven, you're crying, Harry. You're getting my dress all wet. Why on earth are you crying?

HARRY: I'm damned if I know.

ELIZABETH: Then stop it, right now, or you'll have me crying as well.

HARRY: Then do it. Have a good cry.

ELIZABETH: No. Not for you. Not for myself. Neither of us deserves it. *(Pulls away)* I'll be home in time to join you for dinner at the Johnsons'. All this new money needs watching, doesn't it? Meanwhile, have another tot, would you, to stop the pain.

(Exits. HARRY *pours himself another and sings a few bars of* Ta-Ra-Rah-Boom-De-Ay *to himself. Blackout)*

ACT TWO

Scene Four

(The esplanade over the Hudson. A black organ grinder—
JOHNNIE, *in fact—cranks out a tune.* GRANT *is by himself, fumbling in his pockets.* ELIZABETH *approaches.)*

ELIZABETH: I thought I'd find you here.

GRANT: *(Startled)* My dear! I was just watching them excavate for the tomb of some famous ex-President or other.

ELIZABETH: How morbid you've become. Were you looking for a cigar?

GRANT: As a matter of fact, yes.

ELIZABETH: *(Pulling a cigar out of her purse)* Please, then, be my guest. It's your favorite cut of tobacco, isn't it?

GRANT: Yes. Yes, indeed, it is. *(Lighting up)* Were you just out on a stroll, or did you plan to ambush me like this?

ELIZABETH: Let's say I knew you would be here and there is someone I'd like your advice about.

GRANT: Good, I'm ready to give advice, because I can see clearly now that the end is drawing near.

ELIZABETH: General!

GRANT: Of the book, I mean. I got up to page three-hundred-something today, and I'm mostly through the war. Now comes the chapter where Grant meets Lee and so forth. But I'm afraid to write that part, because then it's all over. My publisher here, Sam Clemens, tells me, Don't be scared to finish, General, because that's when you start the next one. Little does he know. There's nothing left after Lee gives up the ghost to Grant.

ELIZABETH: *(Reaching in her purse again)* Here. I brought you some brandy, too.

GRANT: Really? *(Taking the silver flask)* I'm sure this can't be right. What are my vices worth if I can't hide them, and I've tried so hard to hide them from you. I don't think you should give me the permission.

ELIZABETH: I wouldn't fret about it. I might even join you.

GRANT: *(As they share the flask)* General Lee was the most remarkable man, outside of Lincoln, that Grant had ever known.

ELIZABETH: Grant? Grant? Who is this Grant you speak of in the past tense?

(As GRANT continues, CHARLIE drifts on and stops, a little way away.)

GRANT: An historical figure of some little interest, I found out, as I have been writing his life. As for Lee, he was of more interest, dressed in a new uniform for his meeting at Appomattox and carrying a highly polished silver sword. Grant, the poor bugger, had to borrow a uniform off a private in his armies, and, also, he had mud on his boots. Lee said he remembered Grant from the old days. Grant was surprised, because Lee was some sixteen years his senior. Grant said, "What has this all been for?" Lee said, "For supremacy—our poor, backward farming republic against your greater, industrial one. And the colder mind prevailed."

ELIZABETH: That is all old now, isn't it, General, like the Greeks having it out with the Trojans?

GRANT: Ancient. These days, when I finish writing, what I want to do is go out with the girls.

ELIZABETH: But you save your strength, I know, because if you ever became a libertine and didn't finish the great labor of your memoirs…

GRANT: I would leave my family in absolute penury. But I do want the music sometimes, the smell of

ACT TWO

perfume, just once before I can't hear or smell anymore.

ELIZABETH: Yes. So do I. Want it for you. Want it for myself. I am hoping, yes, I am ready.

GRANT: That's odd. So am I.

(CHARLIE *joins them.*)

CHARLIE: Peculiar sight, this. Men and women of society lounging about in public places, drinking strong spirits.

GRANT: Do I owe you money?

CHARLIE: No.

GRANT: Does my touchingly inept son owe you money?

CHARLIE: Not that I know of.

GRANT: Then good day. Unless… (*To* ELIZABETH) This is the Johnny-come-lately you wanted my advice on?

CHARLIE: Advice on me?

ELIZABETH: May we leave it that Ulysses Grant is reputed to be a fine judge of character?

CHARLIE: Leave it anywhere you like.

ELIZABETH: You see his manners, General. The gentleman is from Detroit.

GRANT: I know where he's from, Bessie. And he knows me. I buried his father in the great war. On the other hand, when we met a while back at one of Mrs Fish's flossy Newport rowdedows, I don't believe I had the chance to form much of an impression of his character.

CHARLIE: Though I am a great admirer of yours, General. I know you botched up pretty well the job of being President, and you've had some bad luck since in the banking business, but you were, as my father wrote to my mother in one of his last letters, the brightest star in the firmament when you engineered our victory over the slave-holding South, and you yourself, no matter what your Cabinet did, never stole a nickel from the public treasury.

GRANT: Thank you. You must be sure to buy my book, which will be published soon. You must be sure all your friends buy it, as well, and their friends, too, and their friends' friends' friends'... *(To* ELIZABETH*)* I know where this is going, Bessie. And I know where I'm going, too. My face hurts something awful.

ELIZABETH: Shall I walk you back?

GRANT: Hell, no. That's my driver over there, and I'm sure you have more important things to do. *(Sotto voce)* He seems okay to me. A little abrupt, but honest.

ELIZABETH: Bless you, sir.

GRANT: No, bless you. We must take in the vaudeville next week some day. I've discovered it's a fine painkiller. *(To* CHARLIE*)* Good day, young man. Be sure you remember that you are in company with an extraordinary woman, and if you even for a moment take that for granted, grant yourself that you will have to answer to Grant. *(Exits)*

CHARLIE: An extraordinary woman. Does he really believe all that nonsense?

ELIZABETH: You think I'm not?

CHARLIE: I think you have qualities.

ELIZABETH: Like a well-tuned motor? That's not much of a greeting.

CHARLIE: We've seen each other, remember, but once.

ELIZABETH: But your letters...! I've read and reread them I don't know how many times.

CHARLIE: Well, I should tell you, first off, that those are the kinds of letters I learned how to write when I was a

ACT TWO 65

young man. In fact, I studied how to write those kinds of letters. They are very flowery in places—and contain sentiments that other men who are more romantic than myself might have made seem unique.

ELIZABETH: Do you mean what you wrote is not you?

CHARLIE: Not at all. The letters are what I would call my soul. But there's more to me than my soul, and it is very businesslike.

ELIZABETH: A pity. I am not businesslike at all. I would hate to have to understand and manage everything. Do you think I shall have to learn how?

CHARLIE: It would be better for you, in the long run.

ELIZABETH: The long run...! *(Suddenly trembles)* Oh, heavens, I've just had a chill of some kind. Please, hold my hand. No one is looking.

CHARLIE: *(Taking her hand)* Better?

ELIZABETH: So much the better, now I can feel that you have warm blood flowing in you. You know, all the while I studied your letters, I wondered, was this strange man from Detroit, Michigan, really a sort of giant who had taken it upon himself to rescue me from my little life?

CHARLIE: You sound like you're afraid of me?

ELIZABETH: Oh, my, yes. You write about a very frightening kind of life.

CHARLIE: It's only a different kind.

ELIZABETH: But why should I, if I cared to, want to join you?

CHARLIE: Because it is the future, Miss Elizabeth. Less the exhausted kind of refinement one finds in the East, but its own kind of poetry.

ELIZABETH: In some kind of machine, I suppose, that flies like a bird?

CHARLIE: Why not?

(The organ-grinder returns and cranks out a dreamy waltz.)

ELIZABETH: Well, you do dance, don't you, or isn't that very businesslike, either?

CHARLIE: I dance.

(And CHARLIE and ELIZABETH do, in a most perfect, slow, and stylish way.)

ELIZABETH: Do you also make love to women?

CHARLIE: All the time.

ELIZABETH: *(Mock shock)* Oh, no! Really? I feel terrible!

CHARLIE: Why?

ELIZABETH: Because I'm having such a good time with a man who is so worldly. I'll bet you've broken half a hundred hearts.

CHARLIE: Twelve, I think. Maybe thirteen. And you've broken how many?

ELIZABETH: Women like me don't break hearts.

CHARLIE: Except your own.

ELIZABETH: Oh, you are so cold! You are such a cold-hearted man. How could you have written me such spiritual letters?

CHARLIE: *(Stopping her with a kiss)* Because you may be too valuable to lose. Is it really so important to keep up appearances with these people while you dream about another life you might have…

ELIZABETH: Or, should I run away with you, into some sort of reasonable transcendence?

CHARLIE: Well, it does sound awful when you put it like that.

ELIZABETH: What other way can I put it? Why don't you kiss me again, to see if I can get another angle on it?

(CHARLIE *does.*)

CHARLIE: And now?

ELIZABETH: Charlie, I liked the kiss well enough, but it confused me. It made me want you in ways I used to consider unacceptable. But will I go crazy, then, while you remain sensible and orderly? I could follow you anywhere, but I dread the outcome. I know I will end up going to hell because I shall have hurt so many people. My mother will drop dead, Harry will drink himself to death, no one I now call a friend will ever speak to me again, and I will be cut loose to drift. At your side, of course, but to drift, to try and find my own way. And all I can see, when I think about it, is the terrible morning sometime in the future when I wake up and look at you, or you wake up and look at me, or we both have the same awakening, and we don't like what we see. We stare at each other and say nothing. And so we separate and start again, both of us set adrift—because that is the way things happen nowadays, that we don't stick by anything anymore once we've figured it out. *(Pause)* I don't want my life ever again to depend on one person alone, especially one man.

CHARLIE: That must be the stupidest statement I ever heard from an intelligent woman.

ELIZABETH: *(Confused by her feelings)* Do you think so? Well, I think I've got to go home now.

CHARLIE: *(Suddenly uncool)* No, Elizabeth, Bessie... please! I am serious!

ELIZABETH: So am I! *(Sudden fury, beating on his chest)* I don't want to have to care about you so much!

(The organ-grinder sidles up with his tin cup.)

ELIZABETH: Pay him something for our pleasure, sir!

(As CHARLIE drops a coin, ELIZABETH looks at the organ-grinder.)

ELIZABETH: Johnnie! Johnnie Goodenough! What are you doing here!

(As JOHNNIE tips his hat, ELIZABETH runs out.)

(Blackout)

Scene Five

(A loud banging on a distant door and then lights up on MRS ASTOR, who sits alone, ramrod straight, in her drawing room. HARRY, in disheveled evening clothes, enters, a little wobbly on his pins.)

HARRY: I know it's very late.

MRS ASTOR: Ah, Mister Lehr, come in.

HARRY: I've been walking the streets, and I couldn't think where to go. You see, there's no one home at my house.

MRS ASTOR: You are always welcome here. But, please, you needn't feel so melancholy. She'll be back, all right, your darling Elizabeth. A girl must visit her mother, from time to time. I know I had to.

HARRY: It's just that I am desperately uncertain as to why she would return to Philadelphia. She's never wanted to do that before. But, these days, she's gotten so restless.

MRS ASTOR: Oh, really?

HARRY: It seems that she's met a man who used to sail boats around here when he was a lad, and now he revisits, from time to time, to dip his oar in. I don't see him as much of a challenge. I mean, he works on crazy ideas like the gasoline carriage and such stuff. But he hates us, I know, and, all we stand for, and because of that, I suspect, Elizabeth is quite enthralled with him.

MRS ASTOR: I wouldn't be too hasty about drawing any conclusions. She was brought up in the proper fashion, wasn't she? She knows her limits.

HARRY: I will try, as always, to heed your advice. But now I truly rattle around in that big house of ours, because I seem to have lost my manservant, as well. He ran off in the middle of the night and left no notice.

MRS ASTOR: My dear, is it serious? Were you close to him?

HARRY: No, no, not at all.

MRS ASTOR: Then I shouldn't let it bother you.

HARRY: But I'm afraid of what he knows about me. You understand, the little things a man does, once in a while…

MRS ASTOR: It is sad, of course, to lose a confidant. But within our circle, no real harm comes. No one is born, he or she arrives. No one dies; he or she passes quietly on. And no one can ever be evil. Bad, yes, or make a mistake, but evil is out there, Mister Lehr, far beyond my door. Do you understand what I am saying?

HARRY: But I have been unfaithful.

MRS ASTOR: Oh, yes? That doesn't strike me as something I need to know, unless you have been unfaithful to me.

HARRY: Never.

MRS ASTOR: Good. I am the only woman I know who has not, shall I say, wandered a little, and that is because I don't care enough, I simply don't. You be as careful as may be and remain close and we shall protect you.

HARRY: I'm surprised this doesn't matter to you.

MRS ASTOR: Oh, it matters, and I'll remember... everything. It all goes to show, however, that you are frail. All people, my friends, my enemies, are frail, one way or the other. Only I am not. *(Pause)* When you go home tonight, look once or twice at your wife's picture. Forget this valet of yours. And, if possible, try and do nothing after midnight you wouldn't like known by the dawn's early light.

HARRY: Yes, thank you. Thank you for everything. It's just that I am so lonely now.

MRS ASTOR: We all are, my dear. It is the condition of greatness. *(Pause)* Now, if you might, I would like to hear just one simple melody from your golden throat before I retire.

HARRY: Of course. I live for these moments, do I not?

MRS ASTOR: Indeed, one hopes.

HARRY: *(With sudden and dazzling clarity)* A little maiden climbed on an old man's knee, Begged for a story— "Do, Uncle, please. Why are you single? Why live alone? Have you no babies? Have you no home?"
"I had a sweetheart, years, years ago;
Where that's gone, pet, you will soon know.
List to the story, I'll tell it all— I believed her faithless, after the ball.

(MRS ASTOR, *who has fallen asleep, snores gently.* HARRY *is alone.*)

HARRY: After the ball is over, after the break of morn,
After the dancers' leaving, after the stars are gone:
Many a heart is aching, if you could read them all,
Many the hopes that have vanished, after the ball....

ACT TWO   71

(Blackout)

Scene Six

(On the veranda of her home, Mrs Drexel *dozes. Next to her, bundled in a blanket,* Grant *also sleeps.* Elizabeth *enters and puts her hand gently on her mother's shoulders.)*

Mrs Drexel: *(Awakening)* Oh, my heavens…!

Elizabeth: Shush, shush, mother. We mustn't wake the General. It is all I could do to get him out of the city and into the country for some rest.

Mrs Drexel: Was it only your concern for his health that brought you home after such a protracted absence?

Elizabeth: It was time we spoke.

Mrs Drexel: Be careful. It may not be my time.

Elizabeth: Then you are much as you were?

Mrs Drexel: They tell me I am better than I seem. I know I am worse. They tell me, however, to remain calm. One little shock might be enough to push me over the edge and into eternity.

Elizabeth: Where you are confident you shall inherit bliss.

Mrs Drexel: "Confident" would be a presumption. I have committed my share of sins.

Elizabeth: The greatest of which would seem to be that you have let yourself be in ill health for so long.

Mrs Drexel: What a queer thing to say.

Elizabeth: *(Looking at some views through a stereoscope)* Niagra Falls. It is so close.

Mrs Drexel: Though my various constitutional weaknesses are directly attributable to some overreaching in my youth. I danced too much. I stayed up late too many nights running. I had, also, a fondness for flowers and some varieties of red wine. *(Pause)* And I lied to my mother. Often.

ELIZABETH: *(About another view)* The Brooklyn Bridge. I can almost smell the cabbage boiling in those rundown little tenements.

MRS DREXEL: Then there was the dalliance with Mister Fredericks of South Philadelphia, who attended Yale with the poor Astor boy who died of typhoid fever. When I finally told Mister Fredericks that I couldn't possibly love him as much as he loved me, he hanged himself right out back of our house, from an old apple tree which grew there.

ELIZABETH: You've never told me this before. And was he really so awful, this gentleman you had to turn down?

MRS DREXEL: No. Many people thought him the catch of the season. He was certainly good-looking and he had a grand fire to him—a busy, busy young man. He was always seeing into the future, always afraid it would overtake him unless he stayed on top. I can still see him standing in the back of our old house in a dreadful rainstorm, shaking his head in disbelief when I told him I would not have him, and him shouting back, with that voice of his, You are afraid! And I told him, I most certainly am not!

ELIZABETH: But you were, weren't you, terribly afraid. What if you *had* married him?

MRS DREXEL: It wouldn't have succeeded, I feel positive. He was not acceptable to my parents. But he did bring me the most beautiful bouquets of flowers.

ELIZABETH: And so he's held onto your heart all this time.

ACT TWO

MRS DREXEL: Would you stop it?

ELIZABETH: No. I think you loved this doomed Mister Fredericks much more than you ever cared for my father, is what I think.

MRS DREXEL: He was just a man, one of many. This conversation is unbearable.

ELIZABETH: I'm sorry.

MRS DREXEL: In a pig's eye, Bessie. You've become coarse and unfeeling.

ELIZABETH: I know how it must have been for you—is all I meant.

MRS DREXEL: Do you really?

ELIZABETH: Mr Fredericks stood in the light of the lamp by the stable as the rain poured down on him, and he begged. And you didn't think it was right, a man should beg a woman.

MRS DREXEL: Yes, but his words went right through and into me. Never had any human being seemed so utterly without defense. I raised my hand, I lowered my hand, I fluttered my hand in the air, so he wouldn't see that there were tears in my eyes. And I told him, It could never work out between us. He asked if I were so very sure about that. I said I was. He kissed me once or twice or maybe three times and turned and walked away and was gone from sight in the downpour, which I imagine kept falling on him as he trudged on, over the path, through the trees, to the muddy road, kept pouring on him as he got near the crossroads and stood helpless outside the inn, poured into every pocket and sleeve and cuff of his thin suit as he thought, I can have it all but her, poured steadily down as he shed his wet clothes and tried, as I tried that night, to sleep, just one good sleep, the water endlessly pouring down on us, and everywhere around us…

ELIZABETH: My dear mother. All this long, long time.

MRS DREXEL: There is someone else is your life, too, isn't there? Another fellow who hovers around in your head every time you look at Harry?

ELIZABETH: Yes.

MRS DREXEL: And you think you love him more?

ELIZABETH: That's how it seems to me. I don't know if he is a great man, but he's very glamorous because he is so different.

MRS DREXEL: Has he brought you beautiful bouquets of flowers yet?

ELIZABETH: Good heavens, no!

MRS DREXEL: He will. And so, here you are, considering a divorce, the one thing I have always forbidden my children, and you've come home to ask my blessing.

GRANT: *(Suddenly stirring)* Goddamnit, give her your blessing.

ELIZABETH: General. Please don't fuss.

MRS DREXEL: Yes, please, Ulysses. We were only hashing out family matters.

GRANT: That's very much the vogue now, isn't it, talk everything interesting to death? Well, we were all kept down for so long in our generation, and now we get to move around everywhere and so we've lost our children and we've lost our homes. Still, we must think of what's best for the children. Don't mind me, though. I was just now having this strange dream in which Abe Lincoln, looking as puzzled and weary as he did in real life, was telling me, Grant, damn it all, we've got to go back and pick up where we left off—it's not over yet, the black and white thing. And there I was, just about to say to him, No, sir, nor will it ever be—when I heard

ACT TWO 75

the two of you squabbling. So, I'm going back now, see if I can settle this matter with the President... *(And falls back to sleep)*

MRS DREXEL: Ulysses...?

ELIZABETH: The woods here used to be filled with wild bears and poisonous snakes. Now they've all moved to the city.

MRS DREXEL: Elizabeth, do what you believe is right.

ELIZABETH: I will try to, of course.

MRS DREXEL: But, please, understand that with every breath I have left in me, I disapprove.

ELIZABETH: This is so very hard for me, too.

MRS DREXEL: I imagine it is.

(ELIZABETH kisses her mother, then exits.)

MRS DREXEL: Ulysses? Ulysses! *(Takes his hand)* Dear Lord, when you're gone and I'm gone, what will be left of us?

(Blackout)

Scene Seven

(HARRY lies unconscious in a bed behind which giant windows rise. MRS FISH sits by his side.)

MRS FISH: *(Putting a cloth on his brow)* Harry, you had better pull out of this one, do you hear me? Harry?

HARRY: *(Sitting up suddenly, singing with manic speed)*
Ta-ra-ra boom-de-ay,
Ta-ra-ra boom-de-ay,
Ta-ra-ra boom-de-ay,
Ta-ra-ra boom-de-ay...
(Falls back again, instantly unconscious)

MRS FISH: My dear, this will not do. You've got to get up. You may not be aware, but everything is falling apart around us and Newport has gone to the dogs this season. Women are wearing shorter skirts and a number of them have been observed smoking cigarettes in public. Several prominent men have cut off their wives' discretionary funds, as the entertainment budget is now called. And that's because, I know for a fact, two very famous businesses are bankrupt and a dozen others are under suspicion. And, to top it all, would you believe—the other Mrs Astor, Alva Belmont, who made such a stink about her divorce, was seen leading a suffragette parade down High Street? Alva with a vote? God help us! Get up, Harry, rise from your bed! The time is ripe, as never before, for satire!

(ELIZABETH *enters.*)

ELIZABETH: How is he?

MRS FISH: Unchanged. That is what his doctor said. I mean, I believe you should have been here to talk to his doctor, not me.

ELIZABETH: Harry has treated himself very badly.

MRS FISH: He will rally to fight another day.

ELIZABETH: Good. When he wakes up again, I have something to tell him.

MRS FISH: I will not let you give him any bad news, Mrs Lehr.

ELIZABETH: Why not? It is my husband. It is my news.

MRS FISH: *(Suddenly dead serious)* Because Harry is dying.

ELIZABETH: And how long do you think that might take?

MRS FISH: You are a cold fish, I must say.

ACT TWO

ELIZABETH: As cold a fish as you, Mrs Fish?

MRS FISH: Much colder. As for Harry, one can never tell with these sorts of things. He could linger for years. I hope he does. Because when Harry dies, a certain fire will have gone from our lives and he will be replaced by simply ordinary lick-spittles and bottom-feeders. So, there will be no one left anymore who can show them what giant fools they all are.

ELIZABETH: But are you not one of them yourself?

MRS FISH: Bessie, lead whatever other life you have to quietly. But, do the decent thing, stick by Harry.

ELIZABETH: I have tried, Mamie, believe me. For so long, I have tried.

MRS FISH: *(Embracing her)* I know, my dear.

HARRY: *(Waking again)*
A smart and stylish girl you see,
Belle of good society,
Not too strict, rather free,
Yet as right as right can be—
(Getting out of bed)
Will no one here join me?

MRS FISH: *(Into* HARRY's *giddy mood)* Why? Are you coming apart?

HARRY & MRS FISH:
Ta-ra-ra boom-de-ay,
Ta-ra-ra boom-de-ay,
Ta-ra-ra boom-de-ay,
Ta-ra-ra boom-de-ay—

MRS FISH: *(Ending it)* And ta-ra-ra the rest of it. You must save your strength, Harry.

HARRY: But it was so sweet, my friends, it was like a glass of cold champagne. Do you suppose I could get a glass of cold champagne, by the way, and one each, please, for yourselves?

ELIZABETH: Harry, is your mind clear just this moment?

MRS FISH: Don't answer that!

HARRY: Yes. Well, no. Well, perhaps. It comes and goes. Mustn't let that get around, by the way. On the other hand, if I were a little ga-ga, who'd notice in this crowd anyway, eh?

ELIZABETH: I am leaving you.

HARRY: Are you? When will you be back?

ELIZABETH: You will have your money, still. I'll pay that. You will have the house.

HARRY: I don't want the house. I've never liked the house.

MRS FISH: Harry, dearest, would you like to go for a drive? I have my coach outside.

HARRY: I would love to go for a drive. Just let me bundle. *(Grabs the quilt off the bed)* Will you come with us, Bessie?

ELIZABETH: I am going to pack.

HARRY: Oh, yes, please. But not too much. You'll be back, you know. We're not that sort of people.

MRS FISH: We are not, indeed.

ELIZABETH: Harry, I would like you to understand what I am doing.

HARRY: Why?

ELIZABETH: Because we have known each other so long that I think of you, very often, as my friend.

HARRY: I have no friends. *(To* MRS FISH*)* I think Bessie will reconsider, she usually does. Mamie will flourish and think of a new prank. And Harry, well, Harry will have some more champagne, but in moderation now. As long the money lasts, isn't that right? That's the way it's always worked. Your arm, Mrs Fish?

MRS FISH: I would be so delighted, Mister Lehr.

HARRY: And I will see you for dinner, Mrs Lehr.

(HARRY *exits with* MRS FISH. ELIZABETH *sits on the bed, letting down her hair.* CHARLIE, *hands behind his back, enters.*)

CHARLIE: The two of them said hello to me on the stairs, but they had no idea who I was.

ELIZABETH: *(Running to embrace him)* Charlie!

CHARLIE: Careful, careful, you'll crush these. *(Produces a bouquet)*

ELIZABETH: My mother told me you would bring me flowers.

CHARLIE: She did? What else did she say?

ELIZABETH: That she disapproved, I believe her words were, "with my every breath".

CHARLIE: Good for her.

ELIZABETH: Charlie…!

CHARLIE: Well, it wouldn't be any fun, would it, if it were too easy? And old Harry?

ELIZABETH: Old Harry won't take me seriously, because we've lived as we have for so long. He is going to die, anyway. So let him die, for all the good he ever did me. Ta-ra-ra-boom-de-ay!

CHARLIE: You can't do this, can you?

ELIZABETH: Oh, you think not?

CHARLIE: I know you are not the sort of person deep-down who can suddenly make her heart hard against all the things that have mattered in the past.

ELIZABETH: Wrong, Charlie. And that is why you find me deciding to do a deed unheard-of-before in my family and dangerous, both, and I want so much to live through it without being completely swept up in any more falsehoods.

CHARLIE: And how, may I ask, do you plan to avoid even the occasional deception?

ELIZABETH: With your help.

CHARLIE: It could be, though, that I am not as sturdy and reliable as you have built me up to be.

ELIZABETH: Probably not. But you are a brand-new sort of man, and, in this time when everything has a gold coat on it, you have a soul of iron. A good, honest type of soul.

CHARLIE: Well, I don't mean to be honest. I just can't help myself.

ELIZABETH: Oh, we'll both be brave and strong, don't worry. But I want you to know—if you'll forgive me—that once in a while I shall also need an arm around me, a leg, a smile—little touches that speak of a great weakness in me for simple affection.

CHARLIE: Then perhaps, having understood everything in the world there is to be understood, we should try something a bit less complicated?

ELIZABETH: Certainly. Would you be thinking of something sinful?

CHARLIE: It's part of my overall well-considered scheme, yes.

ELIZABETH: Right now?

CHARLIE: Absolutely. And we can steal away from here together in, shall we say, a fortnight?

ELIZABETH: Shall we say a day?

ACT TWO 81

CHARLIE: A week.

ELIZABETH: An hour. *(Pause)* Or did I just imagine you were here?

CHARLIE: Let me see you in old New York, then. I'm sailing a friend's boat back for him. Tuesday next.

ELIZABETH: Yes, Tuesday next. I love you.

CHARLIE: I love you, too.

ELIZABETH: Great day in the morning, don't you think I know that!

(CHARLIE *and* ELIZABETH *fall back onto the bed, flowers flying everywhere and begin to make love.)*

HARRY; *(V O. Dementedly, from the street below)*
Ta-ra-ra boom-de-ay,
Ta-ra-ra boom-de-ay,
Ta-ra-ra boom-de-ay,
Ta-ra-ra boom-de-ay...

(Blackout)

Scene Eight

(MRS ASTOR'S *sitting room, music and noise of a party drifting in from the outside.* GRANT *is seated there as she enters.)*

MRS ASTOR: Ah, Mister President, my people told me you were in here.

GRANT: How do you do, Mrs Astor.

MRS ASTOR: Please, don't get up. My people also told me that you were waiting to see Mrs Lehr.

GRANT: It is imperative that I speak with her at once.

MRS ASTOR: I should hope so. I presume that you intend to correct her misguided course.

GRANT: I have only some news to give her, no advice at all.

MRS ASTOR: Then you ought to. Today is Harry Lehr's birthday. We have planned a surprise party for him. And yet his wife, your friend Mrs Lehr, up and packed her trunks and has a carriage waiting for her at the curb. Her untimely desertion of this fine, if flawed, man is unacceptable.

GRANT: What I have to say to her may throw a shadow over her dreams, but whatever she does ultimately we must allow to be her business.

MRS ASTOR: Not in my house. Not in my world. In fact, I will hold you, and anyone like you, directly responsible if she finally goes ahead with this preposterous plan and bolts the herd.

GRANT: *(Gently, but firmly)* Mrs Astor, I am sorry to say that you are annoying me. I will leave your house as soon as I have spoken with Mrs Lehr.

MRS ASTOR: Please do. And when you go, take your free-thinking ways with you.

(As MRS ASTOR *is exiting,* HARRY, *dressed up like someone's maiden aunt, in grand wig and fine dress, enters.)*

HARRY: Caroline, kindness stops my mouth.

MRS ASTOR: How charmingly you have put yourself together today. *(Exits)*

HARRY: I beg your pardon. Are you not Ulysses Grant, he who was President for a while, and even a general before that?

GRANT: Correct. And you are….?

HARRY: A cousin of Mrs Fish, she who is such a big cheese in the social world. We go back a long way. You know Mrs Lehr intimately, then, do you?

GRANT: We also go back a long way, yes.

ACT TWO

HARRY: Have you known all her husbands in the bargain?

GRANT: She's had but two, one tragically dead.

HARRY: Yes. A fine fellow, I'm told. And the other one, this Harry Lehr?

GRANT: Interesting sort. Not exactly an eager-beaver, but he makes friends easily. Mrs Fish describes him as just one of the girls. I don't suppose, however, I should be talking about him outside his company.

HARRY: No, it's quite fascinating. It sounded like you were writing his obituary just then. So, you think, perhaps, when he passes…

GRANT: Who? Harry Lehr?

HARRY: He is deathly ill.

GRANT: I'm so sorry. But, then, I haven't followed his career all that closely. When I myself must shuffle off this mortal coil, which is probably a lot closer than I can afford to imagine, they'll say—of me, that is Well, we got that part of the history over with, didn't we, and no more trotting *him* out for parades. So, I'd guess, when Mister Lehr passes, they'll also note that the excesses of his generation—you'll pardon me—went with him to the grave.

HARRY: In other words, no more wild parties?

GRANT: I don't know about that. Probably other parties, even wilder than we can imagine…the kind we could never be a part of.

HARRY: Well, we poor old things, damned for being timid.

(Coming over to GRANT *and pulling him to his feet)*

HARRY: Would you care to dance?

GRANT: *(Confused)* I'm in no condition. This isn't the right moment. There isn't even any music!

HARRY: Nonsense. Hear the music in your head. I do. *(As they waltz slowly and awkwardly)* Still, if the world were different, younger, simpler, I might even have fallen in love with you and reformed my silly ways.

GRANT: I don't think so. Women never understood me. Just the men understood me. You're probably better off silly.

HARRY: No, I mean, I would have asked you to forgive me. I would have begged you to do so.

GRANT: Forgive you for what?

HARRY: Say that I had been given a fine opportunity in the world to be respectable and honest and keep the love of a good person and I just let it drift off into a sip of brandy, or a snootful of opium, or even a shameful liaison with a hungry stranger I knew I would never see again. Do I shock you?

GRANT: How would you be all that different from any other soul around here?

HARRY: Then, when all is said and done, you do not think, after all, that I am bad?

GRANT: You may or may not be bad, or secretly very good but wish you were bad. But I'm not perfect myself, and I have no patience left for what you, and people like you, have become.

HARRY: Oh, dear!

GRANT: But I am in pain a great deal of the time now, so you mustn't take what I say too personally, my dear Miss…that is…Mrs…?

HARRY: *(A big dance dip)* Does it matter?

GRANT: Not a whole hell of a lot to me.

ACT TWO

(MRS FISH *enters with* MRS ASTOR. ELIZABETH *hovers just behind. They stop dead when they see what's before them.*)

MRS FISH: *(Quoting herself)*
Oh, Harry, Harry, quite contrary,
How does your garden grow?
With terrapins and champagne corks
And magnums all in a row.
(Pause) Mister President, is that you?

GRANT: *(As* HARRY *moves away)* Mrs Fish.

MRS FISH: Good heavens, I heard you were dead.

GRANT: I heard the same thing myself. *(Pause)* All in all, though, it's been quite pleasant, being dead. Miss…?

HARRY: Agatha.

GRANT: Yes, Miss Agatha, your cousin, she and I just had a nice postmortem visit. Bessie, I really need to have a word with you, immediately. *(To the others)* And in private, if we might?

MRS FISH: So many words in private these days, so many comings and goings. I would really like to put my foot down.

MRS ASTOR: Please, Mrs Fish, don't make a further mess of things. We all know that this will turn out correctly.

MRS FISH: Not if we tiptoe around, it won't. This woman we admitted to our confidence is about to cut out the heart of a man we love and admire.

MRS ASTOR: Nothing can change. Since we have made this new order, things will remain as they were, as they are, as they shall be long after we're gone. Both Mister and Missus Lehr are brilliant enough to know they should not rock the boat.

MRS FISH: So you say. But I really want to make a big stink.

MRS ASTOR: We have spoken.

MRS FISH: No! We should—

MRS ASTOR: And we shall be displeased with each and every person who fails of his or her obligation.

HARRY: Please. I see no reason to spoil this occasion with bad thoughts. Dear Miss Bessie, I hope someday we shall be closer, and what else can I say beside that?

ELIZABETH: Perhaps "bon voyage," my dearest friend?

HARRY: Probably not. Probably never.

ELIZABETH: But, this is goodbye.

HARRY: *(Gracefully, but filled with sorrow)*
We're only these birds in a gilded cage,
A beautiful sight to see,
And...you may think you're happy and free from care,
But you're not, though you seem to be....

(HARRY *gives* ELIZABETH *a small peck on the cheek and exits with* MRS ASTOR *and* MRS FISH.)

ELIZABETH: General, please, don't you, too, draw down on me for what I am about to do.

GRANT: It's not like that a bit. I never had a judgment against you, except that you prosper and be happy.

ELIZABETH: Why all the urgency, then?

GRANT: I was never much good at this, my dear, even in the war. Would you come hold my hand?

(ELIZABETH *does so.*)

GRANT: I must have written a thousand letters like this, if it was one. Always sincere, but always to people I had never met and, God willing, would never have to meet. "Dear Madame and Sir..." —so my formal messages during the war always went— "It is my sorry duty to inform you that your son..."

ELIZABETH: Oh, General, no...

ACT TWO

GRANT: "A brave sailor all his life and having conquered whole oceans, was out in the Atlantic this P M instant, when his vessel was seized by a unexpected squall. All hands escaped tragedy, save the captain, your beloved Charles Edmund, known faithfully to his comrades as Charlie, who was leveled by a falling boom."

ELIZABETH: It can't be...

GRANT: "His mission was an important meeting this Tuesday next in the city, but even his commendable bravery and manifest faith in God could not save him from this sudden and savage caprice of Nature. You have my deepest sympathy and my strongest assurances that he was among the finest of our number. Sincerely yours, Ulysses S Grant, General, United States Army, retired."

ELIZABETH: Dearest Charlie...

GRANT: He was a nice enough fellah, even honorable, perhaps. But where he was concerned, you were selfish. He's the one who died, you know, not you.

ELIZABETH: Then I think I must stop now, stop everything, read my books, do my good deeds, be quiet again, stop it all. Or perhaps, turn back to the river that runs round this little island, look it in the face, then leap over the side and drown.

GRANT: Bullshit you will. Shoot me first!

ELIZABETH: No. We must both hold on. *(Clutching* GRANT's *hands)* Dear friend...! *(Rushes off)*

(Blackout)

Scene Nine

(A bar uptown. A table, some chairs, a black man at the piano. MRS FISH, wearing a three-piece suit and smoking a cigar, enters, pushing GRANT in full Civil War uniform before her in a wheelchair. HARRY, in evening clothes and dark glasses, follows, his hand on MRS FISH's shoulder.)

MRS FISH: This is it!

GRANT: *(Looking around)* My God, what a wonderful place!

HARRY: It smells like a rancid kettle of soup.

GRANT: I love it the more! You know, Grant's devoted family had plans to transport the aging and infirm ex-President and sometime war-hero to his remote mountain retreat in the Catskills. They told him it was to recover his vital spirits. Grant knew it was to die. So he waited until they had all retired for the night and then, like a young child up to no good, he sneaked out of the house...to be with his livelier friends.

(The group finds its place around a table.)

HARRY: I still say it stinks of the slums.

MRS FISH: Whatever you will, my dear, but you all asked to visit someplace very exotic.

GRANT: And I do love it, by all that's holy if I don't! You suppose we could get a drink. I'd really like a drink.

MRS FISH: Do you think you ought to?

GRANT: Aw, it can't hurt my health anymore, and I did finish the damn book!

MRS FISH: Quite right. *(Her best French)* Service! I say, Service!

(The black man—JOHNNIE, in fact—leaves off his piano playing and appears at the table.)

ACT TWO

JOHNNIE: What'll you folks be having?

HARRY: Johnnie?

JOHNNIE: No, sir, we don't have none of that.

HARRY: It is John Goodenough, isn't it?

JOHNNIE: I was asking, What'll it be?

MRS FISH: Well, what do people have in a place like this?

GRANT: You'd be safest with whiskey of any kind.

MRS FISH: I don't drink whiskey. My husband does.

GRANT: Three whiskies, son.

(JOHNNIE *disappears*.)

HARRY: Were you talking to the waiter, Mamie?

MRS FISH: As much as I had to.

HARRY: *(In his sightlessness, excited)* Well, who was he! I have every right to know. One must be very careful of strangers these days! After all, they may be carrying diseases.

MRS FISH: Please, Harry, put on a brave front. Bear all your disappointments in silence just one blessed evening, would you?

(JOHNNIE *returns and puts the whiskies on the table*.)

HARRY: Is that fellow here again?

MRS FISH: He's here again, yes.

HARRY: Make him say something. I want to make sure he isn't somebody I used to know.

MRS FISH: Do shut up now, Harry.

(JOHNNIE *goes back to the piano, where he resumes playing*.)

GRANT: What time is it?

HARRY: *(Fumbling in his pocket)* Could someone read my watch for me?

MRS FISH: *(Doing so)* Five minutes till midnight.

HARRY: The end of the year, poor old thing.

GRANT: The end of the decade, unless I'm mistaken.

MRS FISH: To be more accurate, the end of the century.

GRANT: No, no, that doesn't happen for quite some time. Cheers, then!

HARRY & MRS FISH: Cheers.

(They raise their glasses and drink. MRS ASTOR, *accompanied by* MRS DREXEL, *enters.)*

MRS ASTOR: Really, I am most cross at all of you. To leave me outside in this weather, bundled up against the cold in that carriage with this woman who is the mother of Mrs Lehr and who is completely without conversation at all, while you stop off for a dram of spirits and there are so many other places we could be besides here—it is beyond my comprehension. You have been most rude to me, who commands the rightful attention of so many. What will become of us all and what has been given us to protect and carry forward down to the final generation if we begin to act like schoolchildren whose only ambition is to sneak off and bell the cat? Really.

MRS DREXEL: It was very, very chilly out there, in nigger town.

GRANT: Are you sure you won't be so kind—the both of you—as to join us?

MRS ASTOR: I am sure.

MRS FISH: Then you can bloody well walk home from here, Caroline.

MRS ASTOR: Mrs Fish, shame on you!

ACT TWO

HARRY: Please? We would be most honored, and so, I am sure, would all the other people around us in this room.

MRS ASTOR: Very well. I will sit for one minute, no more.

MRS DREXEL: Against my best instincts, I shall join her.

GRANT: We thank you kindly.

(JOHNNIE *comes over.*)

JOHNNIE: Drink for the new ladies?

MRS ASTOR: No, thank you.

GRANT: One for them and one more each for the rest of us.

HARRY: Johnnie...?

JOHNNIE: Why does he keep calling me that name?

GRANT: There seems to be some controversy in his mind, you see, as to who you are. As we are having the same controversy about ourselves, you are free to join in or leave us alone to settle it quietly. Up to you, really.

JOHNNIE: Yes, sir. (*He goes.*)

GRANT: Do you mind if I ask, has any one of you seen or heard from our dearest Bessie?

MRS ASTOR: You mean Mrs Lehr?

MRS DREXEL: He means my daughter.

HARRY: My wife.

MRS FISH: My God!

MRS DREXEL: Well, I did have a letter from Paris. It seems that Elizabeth has used the rest of her money to buy a small house in a fashionable *arrondisement*. She tells me, beset as her own life has been by failed expectations, that she intends now to lead a retired, and a retiring, life.

MRS FISH: Strange. I heard from a society dame, one of the nouveauest of the nouveaus in the province of Detroit, that a Mrs Lehr had ensconced herself in the most luxuriant of that backwater's fine hotels and was reported, if you can believe it, to be on the streets bright and early every morning, handing out soup and crackers to hungry orphans.

HARRY: No, no, no. That's all quite incorrect. I know myself personally, through a long telegraphic message in which Bessie repeats how devoted she remains to me, that she has tricked herself out in a *pied-a-terre* in San Francisco, where she has adopted Bohemian habits, is seen, she says, with a parrot on her shoulder, and has made friends with a group of brilliant writers who are drinking themselves slowly to death.

GRANT: I had a dream she'd taken up with Abe Lincoln, but that doesn't seem right, does it.

(JOHNNIE *returns, putting down a new round of glasses, including one for himself, which he hoists.*)

JOHNNIE: We don't get many crazy white people in here from downtown, so I thought I'd have one myself with you, if you all don't mind.

GRANT: Mind? I should say the hell not. *(Raising his glass)* Cheers.

ALL: *(Except* MRS ASTOR*)* Cheers!

(All look at MRS ASTOR.*)*

MRS ASTOR: Oh, well, then, cheers!

HARRY: And one hundred years from now, we shall be forgotten. Forgotten, too, will be our love, such as it was.

GRANT: Isn't that the damnedest thing to say.

ACT TWO

MRS FISH: It is. And so we find ourselves here with just one last minute left until midnight.

GRANT: Time to get a start, then. Cheers!

ALL: Cheers!

(All drink. As they do, ELIZABETH *enters and joins them.)*

ELIZABETH: Is this the right place?

ALL: *(Except* JOHNNIE, *variously)* Bessie! Elizabeth! My dear! Mrs Lehr! Darling!

MRS DREXEL: Wherever have you been!

ELIZABETH: I know this is quite improper of me, to drop in like this. And I can't stay long, either. I'm off again soon. But the snow was starting to fall and seeing the famous carriages gathered outside this little claptrap bar, I thought some people I know must be stranded inside. Some old, old friends. And so I sneaked inside the door and paused and watched you and listened.

MRS ASTOR: Do you suppose I could have another whiskey?

GRANT: Take mine, please.

ELIZABETH: But Harry's wrong, you know. Someone will remember us in the future, remember that we were overcome a little by having too much, remember, though, that we had many decent hopes, even if we were ignorant and vain of what we did. But I must tell you, I do hate what's become of us. When I am gone, look to yourselves, look to someone like Johnnie…

JOHNNIE: No Johnnie here. He was never here, never seen in the company of people like you. No, ma'am, Johnnie never knew you. *(Returns to the piano, plays)*

ELIZABETH: I am going away now. Where, exactly, I cannot say yet. But still, I want you to know that it is hard for me to say goodbye because you have all been, for better and for worse, most of the real life I have ever known. But we all knew it couldn't last.

HARRY: You will never be happy out there, my dearest love.

MRS FISH: Although it was not in the cards for you to be happy here, either.

MRS DREXEL: In fact, there is nothing in store for you anywhere. Not the way you are. I learned that about myself quite some time ago.

MRS ASTOR: In that regard, Mrs Lehr strikes me as the pure American girl...

MRS FISH: Innocent...

MRS ASTOR: Rather like a child who never grew up.

MRS DREXEL: A very naughty child.

HARRY: Hoping against desperate hope she will be important.

GRANT: *(Drinking)* Grant's last hours were spent, apparently, seated in a comfortable chair on the porch of his mountain retreat. You see, the way I imagine it, they'd managed to get him up there anyway. He had been reading, so they said, which was getting more difficult for him with every passing day, or perhaps, he just liked to sit there, in the westering sun, and stare back at the travelers who had hiked up to stand goggle-eyed on his lawn, paying him their respects as they might to some old, failing, incomprehensible creature from our more primitive past. In any event, he passed away peacefully and was found something like this.... *(Falls back in his chair, mouth open, arms dangling)*

ELIZABETH: *(Annoyed)* General, wake up! I have to go now. My train leaves in two hours. Won't you say goodbye, please?

ACT TWO

(Suddenly explosion of celebration outside—cannons, church bells, people shouting in the streets)

MRS ASTOR: The New Year, already!

MRS DREXEL: Indeed it is.

MRS FISH: The newest of new years.

HARRY: Cheers!

ELIZABETH: *(About* GRANT*)* See he gets home. You all get home.

MRS DREXEL: I expect you will drop us a line.

ELIZABETH: I will. Remember me, please, from time to time?

(As ELIZABETH *goes,* JOHNNIE *plays and all the others join in singing.)*

ALL: Goodbye, my lady love,
Farewell, my turtle dove,
You are the idol and darling of my heart,
But someday you will come back to me,
And love me tenderly,
So, goodbye, my lady love, goodbye!

(Blackout)

END OF PLAY

www.ingramcontent.com/pod-product-compliance
Lightning Source LLC
Chambersburg PA
CBHW071725040426
42446CB00011B/2225